IN GOD'S GARDEN:

A Devotional
for Gardeners

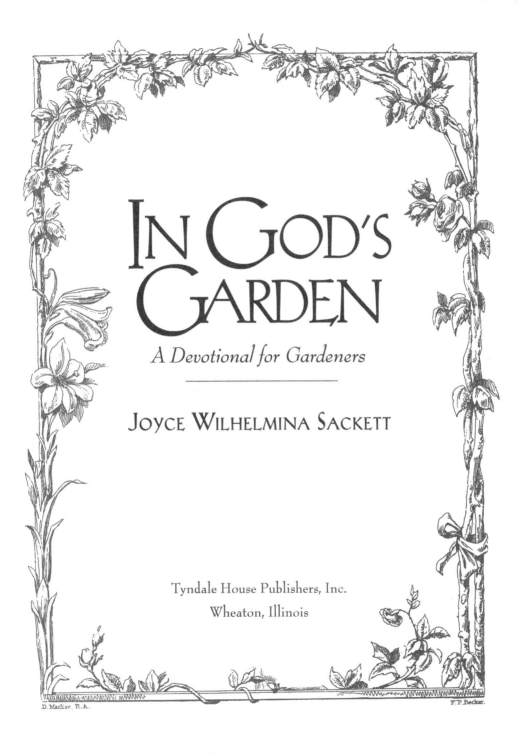

In God's Garden

A Devotional for Gardeners

Joyce Wilhelmina Sackett

Tyndale House Publishers, Inc.
Wheaton, Illinois

D. Maclise, R.A.

F.P. Becker.

Visit Tyndale's exciting Web site at www.tyndale.com

Edited by Linda Washington

Designed by Beth Sparkman

Published in association with the literary agency of Alive Communications, Inc., 1465 Kelly Johnson Blvd., Suite 320, Colorado Springs, CO 80920.

Library of Congress Cataloging-in-Publication Data

Sackett, Joyce Wilhelmina.
  In God's Garden : a devotional for gardeners / Joyce Wilhelmina Sackett.
    p.   cm.
  Includes bibliographical references.
  ISBN 0-8423-5847-1 (hardcover : alk. paper)
  1. Gardeners—Prayer-books and devotions—English. 2. Gardens—
Religious aspects—Christianity—Meditations. I. Title.
BV4596.G36S33 1998
242'.68—dc21   97-35467

Printed in the United States of America

02 01 00 99 98
7   6   5   4   3   2   1

CONTENTS

AUTUMN: *The Garden Gives Gifts*

WINTER: *The Garden Surrenders*

Introduction

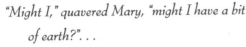

> *"Might I," quavered Mary, "might I have a bit*
> *of earth?". . .*
> *Mr. Craven looked quite startled.*
> *"Earth!" he repeated. "What do you mean?"*
> *"To plant seeds in—to make things grow—*
> *to see them come alive."*
> —*The Secret Garden*, Frances Hodgson Burnett

In Luke 12, Jesus was instructing his disciples: "Look at the lilies and
how they grow. They don't work or make their clothing, yet Solomon
in all his glory was not dressed as beautifully as they are" (v. 27). Jesus
often used the nature he had created to teach spiritual principles. He
would point to plants, flowers, and trees, saying, "Look at that . . .
consider this." He used a common plant in Israel as a metaphor for
himself: "I am the true vine, and my Father is the gardener" (John 15:1).

God's truth is all around us in the garden. He has many things to
teach us there as we work, watch, and think about what we see.

If you enjoy gardening or enjoy the gardens of others, this devotional will encourage you to take a fresh look at the art of gardening and see what you can learn about your spiritual life. The daily readings are followed by questions to help you "dig deeper" into what you've read and guide you in thinking about what God is doing in your life. You'll also find a prayer you can use as is or as a springboard for your own talk with the Lord. Gardening tips are included in a section called "The Gardener's Journal" to help you care for and enjoy your own garden even more.

So, welcome to my garden. May you have pleasure in what you see, and may God instruct your heart as he meets with you there.

SPRING

The Garden Wakes

We wander among divine daffodils framed in a lace-
work of crab apples and along forget-me-not paths
disappearing into flowery glades.

Tovah Martin, *Tasha Tudor's Garden*

Heavenly Sunshine

Jesus said to the people, "I am the light of the world. If you follow me, you won't be stumbling through the darkness, because you will have the light that leads to life."

JOHN 8:12

The daylight is lasting a little longer each day, and I walk around in the garden looking for the green that I lost last autumn. When I spy a leaf pushing up through the soil, I feel like kicking up my heels.

I knew that spring was hiding in the winter garden all along. It was tightly curled inside the gray suede buds on the dogwood. It lay out of sight under the mulch, under a few inches of soil, in swelling bulbs and corms. Now the stirrings of life are everywhere as plants come out of their solstice slumber. The garden is responding to the longer warmer days of spring. It's the sunlight, now more abundant, that gets the new growth going.

God has designed most plants in the world to need sunlight in order to grow, flower, and set seed. These plants convert the sun's energy into food when there is also water and carbon dioxide present. Plants that get plenty of sunlight develop sturdy stems. They become graceful of form and grow to maturity. When plants live in the shadow or are hindered by weeds or too much mulch, they have to make unusual effort to reach the light. They become "drawn"—weak, stretched, and spindly—as they extend and contort to find the sun's rays. Some plants, like sunflowers, dramatically illustrate their need and love of sunlight by keeping their faces turned toward the sun all day long.

People need sunlight, too. Deprived of sunlight, some people fall into a deep depression. All of us feel better when we see the sun and feel it on our skin. And of course, if it were not for the sun, there would be no food and therefore no life anywhere.

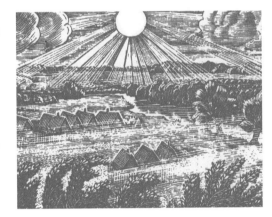

But the light that we need for life even more than the sunlight is the true Light, Jesus Christ. He is the Light the whole world needs, the Light that gives us eternal life. We look at the sun and are reminded of Jesus. We feel the warm rays on our arms in the garden and think of him. He is our sun. His brightness is so much greater than the sun in the sky.

Even if there were no more sun, or if we had no eyesight to see the sunlight, Jesus can light up our heart and mind so we can see and understand eternal things. Time spent with him daily in prayer and reading his Word exposes us to the true Light. Our soul is nourished as the light shines into the corners of our heart. It illuminates the dark places that block his light. As we lean toward this light in confession and praise, the light of God's truth shows us how we need to change and grow.

To follow Jesus, who is the Light of the World, is to discover and do the will of God. Living each day with him is what life is meant to be.

Light leads to life, in the plant world and in our life. Like plants glowing and growing in the warm sunshine, we can bask each day in the heavenly sunshine: Jesus, the Light of the World. ✤

DIGGING DEEPER

What do you usually do when you face a dark time in your life? How can the light of God's love help you in such a situation? How has it helped you in the past? If you're facing a dark time now, consider what you believe about God. Let him strengthen you and encourage you to enjoy your life in him.

PRAYER

Lord Jesus, thank you for driving the darkness out of my life and giving me the light of life. Thank you for the warmth of your reception whenever I come to you for light. Help me to walk in your light. May I be full of your light so that others will see it and come to you for life.

GARDENING TIPS

HERE ARE SOME TIPS FOR LETTING THE SUNSHINE INTO YOUR GARDEN.

TRY PLACING TALLER PLANTS OR CROPS ON THE NORTH SIDE OF THE GARDEN SO THEY DON'T BLOCK THE SUN FROM SHORTER ONES.

PLANT A FEW SUNFLOWERS IN YOUR GARDEN, AND WATCH THEIR FACES FOLLOW THE SUN THROUGHOUT THE DAY. YOUR SUNFLOWERS CAN REMIND YOU TO CULTIVATE THE HABIT OF KEEPING YOUR EYES ON JESUS, THE LIGHT OF THE WORLD. THERE ARE MANY VARIETIES OF SUNFLOWERS. YOU CAN CHOOSE FROM A BROAD RANGE OF HEIGHTS AND COLORS BESIDES THE TALL HAPPY-LOOKING YELLOW ONES. YOU MIGHT CONSIDER CHOOSING A VARIETY THAT COMPLEMENTS THE OTHER COLORS IN YOUR GARDEN.

Planted at His Feet

*There is really only one thing worth being
concerned about. Mary has discovered it—
and I won't take it away from her.*

LUKE 10:42

As the days speed toward spring, I start to feel anxious about garden
duties. How will I get the seeds started in time? And even more urgent,
when will I finally send in the seed order? Most of the bulbs are up, and
some are ready to bloom; yet many are still struggling under a lump of
leaf mulch. I need to take time to rearrange that mulch. Then there's the
general tidying up that needs to happen, like sweeping the terrace, removing blown-down tree branches from the lawn, spreading the compost
around, tilling the *potager* (French for "kitchen garden"), and removing
any debris from last year's garden. I can get so distracted by the growing
to-do list of garden chores that I forget how much fun I'm having!

Someone said, "A garden is a thing of beauty and a job forever!"
And so it is, but I love my job as resident gardener of Blessing Hill.
The work is always pleasant. It just seems to multiply while my time
diminishes.

As the to-do list grows, so do my longings for more plants, more flower beds, one more garden feature that I saw in someone else's garden or in a book. If I give in to the temptation to spend beyond my budget, I am adding to the to-do list; the larger my garden grows, the more work I'll have.

Everyone's life has the tendency to get cluttered with to-do lists. Our days are full of things that insist on our attention, and we cannot deny that many of these things must be done. Yet, according to Jesus, there is only one thing we need to be concerned about— spending time with him. In Luke 10:38-42, Mary discovered this "one thing."

She knew how to remain undistracted from the Lord. She planted herself at his feet, so that she could hear what Jesus was saying. Jesus is so often pictured in the midst of a noisy crowd that we may forget he enjoyed quiet, personal moments with friends. Mary felt secure in this intimate circle, even though she was probably surrounded by men while sitting there at Jesus' feet.

When you hug someone who is wearing perfume, you get some of her perfume on you. Because Mary loved to be near him, she absorbed the likeness of Jesus.

When we grow in our devotion to Christ, spending more and more time with him, the rest of our life will be influenced by those intimate moments with him. Our garden joys and chores will be in their proper place along with the rest of our duties and desires. We will begin to see and do the things that are on Christ's heart because we have been listening to him.

Time spent with Jesus will never be taken away from us. In this way, we build up heavenly treasure, as Jesus commanded (see Matt. 6:20). Our relationship with the Lord here on earth is building a growing friendship with the Son of God that will go with us into heaven.✣

DIGGING DEEPER

Have you made room in your life for times to reflect, to be still and listen to the Lord's voice? When is the best time for you to "sit at Jesus' feet"? Think back to a time when you sat at his feet. How did Jesus speak to your heart?

PRAYER

Father God, David the psalmist wrote, "My heart has heard you say, 'Come and talk with me.'" Like David, "My heart responds, 'Lord, I am coming'" (Ps. 27:8).

Gardening Tips

If you have a large enough garden, consider making a bench where you can sit and enjoy the pleasure of Jesus' company. In Roger B. Swain's book, The Practical Gardener (Boston: Little, Brown and Co., 1989), there is a chapter with diagrams and a materials list for building a simple, inexpensive garden bench.

Consider planting sweet alyssum near your garden seat. Alyssum is an annual and is easy to grow from a seed. The white variety is stronger scented and hardier than the colored types. Alyssum will bloom and perfume the air all summer as you sit in your garden and enjoy the company of the Lord.

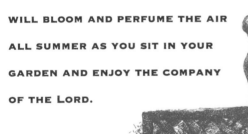

9

The Nature of a Seed, Part 1

*The truth is, a kernel of wheat must
be planted in the soil. Unless it dies it will be alone—
a single seed. But its death will produce many
new kernels—a plentiful harvest of new lives.*

JOHN 12:24

The stuff that garden dreams are made of is arriving in the mail in small cardboard boxes. The seed companies have filled my orders, and I feel rich as I open the boxes and examine the contents—lots of little envelopes full of potential. Each packet contains hundreds of promises that my garden will be the best ever.

I look at my seeds as I plant them and see little dots of gray, tan disks, or small balls of green and brown. I bury them in the ground and wait for the miracle. This process, at once predictable and astonishing, is why we all love to garden. We see that a tiny gray dot of a petunia seed has become a petunia. A bean seed has sprouted into a large plant that produces hundreds of beans. The little tan orbs that we put in a neat row in the garden have become big, beautiful, nourishing spinach plants.

A seed has all the potential for life, but as a seed, it is dead. Nothing is happening inside that hard little kernel. No cells are multiplying. But everything is in place inside that seed to produce something greater than the seed itself. When conditions are suitable and the seed's outer coat absorbs enough moisture to allow the inside kernel to swell, the seed comes to life and bursts out of its coat. Once the seed sprouts and breaks the surface of the soil, I can't see the seed anymore. It is no more. The seed has given itself to become something larger and more wonderful— a plant that will produce many more seeds.

When Jesus said that a seed had to die or it would always be just a single seed, he was speaking of himself (see John 12:23-26). Jesus was that seed that had to die and be buried so that an innumerable multitude could be "reborn" into his kingdom. If he had not died, none of us could ever truly live.

Through this principle, Jesus reminds us that, as his followers, we will have to die, too. How? Through dying to self. We seek the Lord's help each day to choose to do what pleases him, rather than pleasing ourselves. We pray for courage and strength to obey his Word even though it is often difficult and sometimes costly. We learn to say no to any desire that is in conflict with our friendship and fellowship with the Lord. This kind of dying will be different for each of us. As Paul stated, "I have been crucified with Christ. I myself no longer live, but Christ

lives in me. So I live my life in this earthly body by trusting in the Son of God, who loved me and gave himself for me" (Gal. 2:19-20). When we give God our life, he makes it new. He uses each of our lives to affect many other lives

The seed packets that have arrived in the mail are packets full of promise. But I will never smell the flowers or taste the tomatoes unless I bury the seeds in the earth. Our life is like one of those packets, full of unused promises. In order to live, we need to "die": to say no to our own will and yes to his. This death leads to abundant life for us and for all those lives that God will reach through us. ✤

What does "dying to self" mean to you? What are some of the ways God used others to affect your life? In what ways has God used your life to affect other lives? What aspect of your life would you like to share with others?

PRAYER

Lord Jesus, you have asked me to give up my life for your sake and the sake of the gospel. I feel a little afraid sometimes because of what that "giving up" might mean. Help me to focus on your love instead and on the lives you intend to reach through my surrendered life.

GARDENING TIPS

AS SOON AS THE GROUND CAN BE WORKED IN MARCH, USUALLY NEAR OR AFTER ST. PATRICK'S DAY, YOU CAN PLANT PEAS, BOTH EDIBLE AND FLOWERING SWEET PEAS. (IF YOU TILL YOUR GARDEN, LET IT SETTLE A FEW DAYS BEFORE PLANTING.) ALL PEAS LIKE THE COOLER WEATHER OF EARLY SPRING TO GET A GOOD START ON GROWING. SOAKING THE PEAS OVERNIGHT HELPS THEM ALONG IN THE GERMINATION PROCESS.

IVY WILL GROW NICELY INDOORS AND CAN BE TRAINED TO CLIMB AROUND A SUNNY WINDOW TO FRAME THE VIEW.

START SEEDS INDOORS IN MARCH FOR PLANTS THAT WILL GO INTO THE GARDEN IN MAY. USE PLASTIC EGG CARTONS FOR CONTAINERS. CUT THEM ALONG THE FOLD AND USE THE TOP AS A TRAY. POKE A SMALL HOLE IN THE BOTTOM OF EACH SECTION, AND FILL WITH STERILE POTTING OR SEED-STARTING SOIL. FOLLOW DIRECTIONS ON SEED PACKETS REGARDING HOW DEEP TO PLANT THE SEEDS, ONE TO EACH SECTION. THIS METHOD WORKS GREAT FOR ALYSSUM, MARIGOLD, PARSLEY, LETTUCE, AND MANY OTHER ANNUALS.

The Secret of the Garden

This is the day the Lord has made. We will rejoice and be glad in it.

PSALM 118:24

After Easter dinner I walked around in the garden, enjoying what there was to see. I was lifting some leaves off the iris bed next to the stone wall when I uncovered a large fat toad, all warty and brown with shining gold eyes. Actually, we surprised each other. He puffed himself up to intimidate me but I admired him anyway. I showed him to my daughter, and she stroked his back, which he didn't seem to mind. Then I put the leaves back on top of him, hoping he'd stay in my garden in spite of the lack of privacy.

I continued my walk to the corner of the house, where, under a juniper, the Virginia bluebells *(Mertensia virginica)* were already showing their lovely mauve and violet color. I made plans to watch them closely for another week, to see their color change from pinks to blues. There is a magical fleeting time when both colors are visible together.

In her Pulitzer Prize–winning book *Pilgrim at Tinker Creek,* Annie

Dillard wrote, "Beauty and grace are performed whether or not we will see or sense them. The least we can do is try to be there." Being there is what gardening is all about. We want to be there when the tiny beauties open in spring—the scilla and snowdrops, the narcissus, the tiny crimson leaves of the sugar maple, and the bright green frills of flowers on the Norway maple. We want to catch the first glimpse of the fern fiddleheads and the newly opened dogwood buds.

I like the look of buds. When I was younger, I often wanted the process to hurry along, for things to get growing for "real." But now I see that the small starts are necessary and wonderful. There's a timing to it all. If the growth happens too early or too fast, it will be weak or frostbitten. Slow and steady is the usual pace of the garden.

"Today is very seldom like yesterday, if people would note the differences," wrote George Macdonald. This is true of gardens. The secret of the garden is the wonder of the present moment, to notice and revel in it. It is to love what one has, however small, to see in each day's gifts the goodness and greatness of our God. If we are only looking forward to the blossom or the full leaf or pepper that will one day be on the plant, we will miss the beauty that today has to show us. "This is the day the Lord has made. We will rejoice and be glad in it" (Ps. 118:24).

Today, before all is big and full-blown, today, when buds are swollen and light of color, the garden is so lovely.

The flower and fruit are the purpose, we say, of all plant life. We want our plants to grow up. We want the fullness of green in every quarter. Yet we can learn to love the process of growth as well as the result of it. The buds are the true beauty of a spring day.

In the garden, surrounded by the slowly opening buds, I am also surrounded by evidence of the power of God. The ruined and dead garden has been renewed. The buds teach me to watch each day for more evidence of the new life that Christ brings to my life. Each day has been created by the Lord to show me himself, to give me joy, and to cause me to grow in my knowledge and love of him. ✤

DIGGING DEEPER

Psalm 25:14 tells us that the Lord shares his secrets with his friends, those who fear him. What secrets has he shared with you? He has made "today" for you. How will you use this time?

PRAYER

I am perpetually astonished in the garden, Lord. I see so much of your lovely work. Thank you for the beauty of this day. Thank you for the opportunities you give me to praise you for what is and what is to come.

GARDENING TIPS

A MONTH OR SO BEFORE SPRING ARRIVES, YOU MAY CUT BRANCHES FROM FORSYTHIA, PUSSY WILLOW, PEACH TREES, FLOWERING ALMOND, AND OTHER SHRUBS. THE BUDS ON THE BRANCHES WILL OPEN IN A VASE OF WATER ON A WINDOWSILL.

BLUEBERRY BUSHES ARE SHRUBS FOR ALL SEASONS. THEY HAVE BEAUTIFUL BELL-LIKE WHITE FLOWERS IN SPRING, DELICIOUS BERRIES IN JULY, BRIGHT FALL FOLIAGE, AND RED BRANCHES THAT PROVIDE WELCOME COLOR IN THE WINTER GARDEN. BLUEBERRIES NEED ACID SOIL AND FULL SUN TO GROW WELL. KEEP THE AREA WHERE THEY GROW WEED FREE. MULCH AROUND THE BUSHES WITH PEAT OR WELL-CRUSHED OAK LEAVES, COMPOST, OR WOODLAND SOIL. JUST-PICKED BLUEBERRIES WILL KEEP WELL IN THE REFRIGERATOR FOR ABOUT A WEEK. OR PUT THEM INTO FREEZER BAGS AND STORE IN THE FREEZER FOR UP TO A YEAR. THAWED BLUEBERRIES RETAIN MOST OF THEIR PREFROZEN TEXTURE AND FLAVOR.

The Nature of a Seed, Part 2

Oh, that we might know the Lord! Let us press on to know him!

HOSEA 6:3

Little Joyella was recruited to help me, her mommy, plant beans. After I made a long 1½-inch-deep furrow with the corner of the hoe blade, I handed her a bag of white beans. Then I broke a small stick into a three-inch length and gave it to her.

"This is your spacer," I told her. "Here's how you plant the beans: Put one bean down, then lay the stick down in the furrow, with one end touching the bean. Put another bean at the other end of the stick. Just keep moving down the row—bean, stick, bean. See?"

She saw how to do it and planted a whole, long row of beans. It took the better part of the morning, what with the spilling of the beans and taking time out for encouraging hugs.

When Joyella put those beans down in the row, she may have stood them on end or laid them on either side. It didn't matter what position the beans were in. Once I covered them up and watered them, the beans knew what to do.

Every bean and seed has a built-in attitude: "I will grow up." This determination is released as soon as the seed is buried and watered. When I plant a row of peas, I'm so sure they'll obey this inner urge to grow up that I hang netting over the row right after planting, knowing they'll need something to cling to as they climb.

How can we develop that same attitude in ourselves that seeds have—that determination to grow up toward the light? How do we keep alive a desire to get closer and closer to God?

We may ask God for closeness to him. Moses certainly knew God and had seen his power and glory. Yet he hungered for more. He cried out to God, "Let me see your glorious presence!" God said yes to Moses, even though he had to protect him so that he wouldn't die when God's full presence passed by (see Exod. 33:18-23).

God says yes to our request for closeness because he also seeks intimacy with us. He came as close as possible to us in his Son, Jesus Christ. To know Christ is to know God because "the Son reflects God's own glory, and everything about him represents God exactly" (Heb. 1:3).

God's heart is also made visible in the written Word. By reading and memorizing the Word, I am storing the heart of God in my own heart. This causes me to long to know more and more of him.

People get to know each other better through shared experiences. I didn't enlist my daughter's help just to get the beans planted. I wanted to have her near because I enjoy her company. I wanted to share the pleasant experience of gardening with her. I wanted to know her and be known by her.

In the same way, I can know the Lord better by inviting him into all the details of my day, my plans and problems, tasks and fun times. I can determine that I will not hide anything from the Lord but acknowledge him in all I think and do. In this way, I become more aware of the Lord's companionship and guidance.

Because of who the Lord is, we will always find a welcome to intimacy with him. So, let's press on. Let's grow up toward the light and get closer to our Lord. ❖

DIGGING DEEPER

What will you do today to get closer to the Lord, to love, reverence, and praise him? What is your favorite way to spend time with the Lord? How have your times with the Lord affected your life?

PRAYER

O Lord, create in me the longing to be closer to you. Cause me to set my heart and my mind on knowing you better. I thank you that you desire intimacy with me. Cleanse my heart so that I can enjoy your holy presence in my life.

Gardening Tips

Think about planting a variety of beans in your vegetable garden, like the purple bush bean Royal Burgundy. Its stems are purple, and the slender delicious purple bean pods are decorative as they hang in clusters under the leaves. The purple beans turn a dark green when they are cooked.

Scarlet runner beans are easy to grow and will climb fast and high on a pole or on a wall if you help them along with string or netting fixed to the wall. These beans produce lots of bright red flowers that hummingbirds love.

The hyacinth bean (actually a member of the pea family) may be the prettiest of all. All parts of this twining, climbing plant are tinted with purple and will beautify any fence or trellis with its pale purple or white flowers. Its pods are also edible.

Great Day for Dancing

Always be clothed in white, and always
anoint your head with oil.

ECCLESIASTES 9:8, NIV

"Let's celebrate!" That's what Nature seems to be saying every spring. The garden wakes and puts on her party clothes. The trees, still dark and wet from melting snow and rain, dress up in chartreuse frills as the sap climbs high to their branches. The cold, dead earth comes alive with a startling freshness. Pale green points of hyacinth leaves break through the leaf mold. Clumps of narcissus push up small hills of mulch and shake them off as they raise their yellow trumpets and join in the celebration. Red, yellow, and purple tulips arrive and dance in the sun to the music of the breeze. Pansy faces nod in time.

More party decorations arrive in the form of butterflies, fluttering their colors as they dance above the blossoms on sunny days. Leaves, buds, and flowers materialize where they didn't exist before. Every growing thing appears to glow with an inner light.

Gardeners frequently succumb to giddiness because of the phenomenon of spring. It astonishes and thrills us every year. It's no wonder lambs kick up their heels and the days are full of birdsong. Dancing and singing are natural, joyful responses to birth and rebirth. They are expressions of celebration.

What should the gardener wear to the party going on in his garden? The writer of Ecclesiastes encourages us to put some fragrant oil on our face and hair to make us shine as we join in the celebration of life. Wear something white, he says, to express joy and cheerfulness.

On Sundays in Siberia, many young women wear white to church to celebrate the resurrection of Jesus. (The words for *Sunday* and *resurrection* are the same in the Russian language.) After all, on a Sunday, the first day of the week, Jesus Christ rose from the dead and came out of his grave. He was alive and well and seen by hundreds before he disappeared into the heavens, promising to return (see Acts 1:1-11; 1 Cor. 15:3-7).

But before his holy life burst open the tomb, he chose to take upon himself God's punishment for our sins. Almost two thousand years ago, God's Son hung on a cross over the earth, absorbing into himself, even as his blood spilled out, all the sin that could ever keep us from God. Because of Christ's death, we are forgiven, cleansed.

Three days later, by his bodily resurrection, he defeated the death that stalked us all. We now have life, new, abundant, and eternal. Jesus

did what he promised. He turned our mourning into dancing. Such joyous truths start our pulses racing and our feet tapping. We feel like singing.

Long ago, English country people would rise early on Easter morning, hoping to see the sun dance for joy. They were so sure that all creation was celebrating the resurrection of its Creator. I imagine everything in the garden would like to join in the dance, too. The brightness and beauty of the spring garden shouts, "He is risen!" I reply, "He is risen indeed!"

So, when dark clouds loom on the horizon, tell yourself the Good News: "Christ is risen! I'm forgiven!" Then sing about it. Maybe you'll feel like dancing, too! ✤

DIGGING DEEPER

In what ways do you express the joy of your salvation? If you had the opportunity, what words would you use to tell someone about the true significance of Easter?

PRAYER

Lord Jesus, I praise and thank you for your forgiveness, for my salvation, for my life. Thank you for springtime and beauty and joy. Thank you for your love that gives me a reason to celebrate every day.

GARDENING TIPS

THE POET A. E. HOUSMAN (1859–1936), IN HIS POEM "A SHROP-
SHIRE LAD," WROTE THAT THE CHERRY WAS "THE LOVELIEST OF
TREES . . . WEARING WHITE FOR EASTERTIDE." THE PROFUSE BLOS-
SOMS OF CHERRY TREES APPEAR BEFORE THE LEAVES AND LIGHT UP
THE GARDEN FOR WEEKS. SOUR CHERRIES ARE SOMEWHAT HARDIER
THAN THE SWEET VARIETIES AND ARE SELF-POLLINATING. YOU WILL
NEED TO PLANT TWO VARIETIES OF SWEET CHERRIES IF YOU WANT
FRUIT. SEMIDWARF SOUR CHERRY TREES CAN REACH A HEIGHT OF
TWENTY-FIVE FEET.

WHITE FLOWERS ARE LIKE LITTLE LIGHTS IN THE GARDEN
AT NIGHT. THEY ARE THE ONLY
ONES YOU'LL BE ABLE TO SEE
AFTER DUSK. SO IF YOU SIT
OUTSIDE IN THE EARLY EVENING,
PLANT WHITE FLOWERS WHERE
YOU CAN SEE AND ENJOY THEM.
IF YOU CHOOSE WHITE NICOTIANA,
OR FLOWERING TOBACCO, YOU'LL
ALSO HAVE A SWEET EVENING
FRAGRANCE IN YOUR GARDEN.

25

Mulberries Forever

May your roots go down deep into the soil of God's marvelous love. And may you have the power to understand, as all God's people should, how wide, how long, how high, and how deep his love really is.

"Here we go round the mulberry bush, so early in the morning!"

You may have sung this song as a child, but did you ever wonder what type of plant a mulberry bush is? A mulberry bush is really a tree that has been cut down again and again but doesn't die. After each pruning, the tree rises up again with, not one, but *many* branches and sends more roots down deeper into the soil. And why was the tree cut down? Because mulberries grow fast and furious, and their seeds are spread by birds. So you have to dig out the root if you want to get rid of the tree. This is a major undertaking!

You have to start early in the day when it's not too hot. You dig a wide ring around the tree or bush and close in on the root. You dig and dig; by afternoon you hope you got all the bright yellow-orange roots out of the huge hole you've made. Chances are, you probably haven't.

Those mulberry roots hold their ground, and the ground holds them. The ground, or soil, is the mulberry's lifeline, giving it a foothold and providing it food and drink.

Good soil, or loam, is fertile and friable. Its crumbly texture allows water to drain through and air to circulate properly. It is a paradox that loose soil can provide such strong support for roots.

Humans also have a need for strong support of the roots we put down. The apostle Paul tells us to put roots down into the soil of God's love. We are to be like the mulberries, spreading strong roots deep and wide into this soil.

How is God's love like soil? God's love is fully expressed to us in his Son, who showed us what kind of love God has for us. Think of all that Jesus did and said. He touched people and healed them. His disciples were free to lean on his breast and hear his heartbeat. He taught and trained, forgave and prayed, suffered and died and rose again, all for love of us.

God not only loves us, he *likes* us. One of the names God gives to his children is Hephzibah, which means, "My delight is in her" (Isa. 62:4, NASB). We are the beloved children of the one who made the universe. And long before he made anything, God thought of us and chose us to be his because he loved us.

When Jesus told the parable of the sower (Matt. 13:1-23), he spoke about ways the Word of God takes root in a person's life. And what are our roots? They are our affections, our thoughts, longings, gifts, and shortcomings. Our roots are the parts of us that think and choose and love and work. Our roots are our selves. When the Word takes root within us, we then begin to change.

When we know we are loved, we can relax because we do not need to make an "impression." We are free to grow spiritually because our hunger for significance and security is satisfied by the extravagant and accessible love of God. When we know we are loved, we are able to love others. ❖

DIGGING DEEPER

What can you do to more fully accept and respond to God's love? What effect do you think the extravagant, eternal love of God can have on your self-image? Is there someone you know who needs to hear about the strong and tender love of God? If so, how will you share God's love with that person?

PRAYER

Dear Father, help me to respond to your love with all that I am. Show me how to put my roots down deeper in your love. Thank you, Lord, for telling me in so many ways every day that you love me. I love you.

Gardening Tips

Worms are called "nature's ploughmen" because their burrowing in the earth helps aerate the soil and aids drainage. Worms leave humus—digested organic material—behind as they tunnel through the soil, which helps the soil hold water. Roots digest the humus left behind by the worms and take in the air that flows there.

If your soil is rocky or too clayey, add humus, that dark brown, crumbly, sweet-smelling decomposed vegetation your compost pile will eventually become. Other kinds of humus include rotting straw, peanut hulls, peat moss, and any decomposed vegetation. Humus will loosen up the soil and make it inviting to worms, which will continue the job of keeping the soil in good condition.

May I Introduce . . . ?

*I will give to each one a white stone, and on the
stone will be engraved a new name that no one
knows except the one who receives it.*

REVELATION 2:17

What's in a name? Consider the daisy. Why do we call it a
daisy? Because some species of this flower close their blossoms
at night, people in England centuries ago called it *day's eye.* Gradually the pronunciation was condensed into the one word we use
today—*daisy.*

And what about the pansy? "There is pansies, that's for thoughts,"
wrote Shakespeare. The name for this little flower with a face that
looks like it's frowning or thinking comes from the French word for
"thought"—*pensée.* Some varieties of pansies have intriguing common
names: heartsease; Johnny-jump-up; kiss-me-quickly.

Throughout history, people have given common and scientific
names to plants, flowers, shrubs, and trees. The common name of
a plant is often a term of endearment or an astute observation of a
plant's nature. This name may change from one part of the country

(or world) to another. The scientific name is usually Latin or Greek with a Latin ending and is the same all over the world.

The first word in the Latin name states the genus or family of the plant. For example, the sugar maple's Latin name is *Acer saccharum.* The second word tells something about the plant's form or growth habit. You can recognize several common words in these plant names: *fragrans* (smells good) and *multiflora* (many flowers) or *foetidus* (smells bad) and *horrida* (has dangerous spines).

Some plants are named after the people who discovered or developed them. Some unique quality of the plant is hidden in its name. Every plant name has a story to tell.

Like plants, people have been given two names, too. What I call our "common" name is the one by which we are known on earth. This name may be from our ancestors or may tell something about our parents' hopes for us. Our name might also have been the popular choice the year we were born.

Revelation 2:17 tells us that we will be given a new name when we go to live with our Lord in eternity. This name will tell the truth about who we are. It is a picture of our soul, a private, intimate name known only to God and us.

As you can see, names are important to God. His own name is sacred. The book of Isaiah tells us that God knows all the billions of stars by name. Each star is special to him in some way. He knows it and has named it. And all people are known to God by name. We are not just a multitude, but individuals dear to him with unique characteristics, gifts, strengths, and weaknesses.

Perhaps a part of our new name is being formed as we live out the Christian life on earth. As we use our gifts for God's glory and persevere in spite of our weaknesses, God lets us help him write the stories that our new names will tell.

The name that he will give each of us in heaven will also reveal to us what God thought of us when he first made us. It will show how much he loves us and how intimately he has known us all along. ✤

DIGGING DEEPER

Do you like your name? How do you think it describes you? If you could give yourself a new name, one you would be known by forever, what would it be? What does this new name describe about you?

PRAYER

I worship you, Lord God, for creating people as individuals— each one different, each one known intimately by you. I thank you for creating me with the capacity to know you intimately, too. And I look forward to the time when we will share the secret of my new name.

Gardening Tips

Labeling the plants in your garden is a good practice. Just the common name or the scientific name is enough on the label. Then, in your gardening journal, you can record this name, the date you bought the plant or planted it, and any other facts about it.

Labels will help you to learn your plants by name. The labels may be hidden among the foliage, or they may be a more obvious and attractive part of the garden's design. A pretty way to show a plant's name is to paint it on a smooth stone with oil paint. River stones are best, with their smooth, pale surfaces. Choose stones that are at least three by four inches or whatever size you like. This is a specially nice treatment for an herb garden.

If seeds in the black earth can turn into such beautiful roses, what might not the heart of man become in its long journey toward the stars?
—G. K. Chesterton

SUMMER

The Garden Grows

How good it is to see the brilliant light of the blessed
summer day, and to feel one's own thankfulness of
heart, and that it is good to live, and all the more good
to live in a garden.

Gertrude Jekyll, *The Making of a Garden*

The Perfect Gardener

I will ask the Father, and he will give you another Counselor, who will never leave you. He is the Holy Spirit, who leads into all truth.

JOHN 14:16-17

The neatly printed notice on the grocery store bulletin board read: "Retired estate gardener; will work for the love of it if the garden meets approval; requires a sandwich and a cool drink at noon; has own tools."

I called the phone number listed, sure that this incredible person was already snatched up. But he wasn't. He arrived dressed in a light blue shirt, overalls, and cap. He seemed much older than I, but he had a vitality I hadn't seen in younger help. His manner was polite yet authoritative. In a clipped British accent, he told me that he was ready to tour the grounds to see if he would take the job. I guess he liked what he saw, or what he thought he could do for my garden, because he decided to work for me.

Every day I gave him a list of things I wanted done, which he completed. He knew how to dig, how to prune, how to move a tree. He was strong, experienced, wise, and alert to the needs of each plant, calling them by name. I followed him around and became his pupil. He understood my vision for the garden and added much to it without seeming to undermine my ideas. Everything in the garden responded to his touch. He may have tended other gardens, but he gave mine his full attention five days a week.

This happy arrangement continued for quite a while—until I woke up from my dream.

Of course, such a perfect gardener doesn't exist except in novels and dreams. Also, many gardeners don't want anyone else in their gardens. They prefer to do all the work themselves. This may be a good way to garden, but it is not a good way to grow in our spiritual life. We need help.

God has given his children a resident tutor, who is committed to helping us along to spiritual maturity. The Holy Spirit, a gift from Jesus, has taken up residence within us. He is our teacher, our guide, our encourager. His goal is to help us become more and more like our Savior.

The Spirit of God brings us the truth straight from heaven. He helps us to remember and love Jesus' words, to begin to think like Jesus thinks. He is our source of all knowledge. The many and diverse talents and skills that are in the body of Christ are all gifts of the Spirit. He teaches us to appreciate and celebrate these gifts and to use our own to serve others.

The gardener who daily observes the needs and troubles of each plant can solve a problem fairly quickly. Because he is right there in the garden every day, he can nurture and preserve the beauty he enjoys. If we have received the salvation Jesus offers, his Holy Spirit—our perfect helper—

is permanently present in us. He is involved in whatever is happening to us. If we are willing to listen and follow him, he will teach us to live a fruitful and beautiful life, worthy of Christ's name.

Near my home is a famous garden tended by a team of dedicated gardeners. It is beautiful every day of the year. On a hill in this

garden there is a small temple that looks out over acres of loveliness. This scene reminds me that my life is tended by the Lord personally and perfectly, as if I were his garden. After all, I am—as are you—the temple of his Holy Spirit. ❖

DIGGING DEEPER

How do you feel knowing that God indwells you by his Spirit? When have you experienced his comfort or his instruction? Think about a specific time.

How can you be more conscious of his presence and work in you? (See Romans 8:1-17.)

PRAYER

Lord God, I want to be in tune with your Spirit living in me. Teach me to listen to and follow him. Thank you for the wonderful gift of your constant presence and encouragement.

GARDENING TIPS

THE WORD <u>MANURE</u> MAY SEEM UGLY, BUT IT'S PRETTY TO GARDEN-ERS BECAUSE OF ITS USEFULNESS. RABBIT MANURE IS THE ONLY KIND THAT IS SAFE TO APPLY FRESH TO THE GARDEN IN SPRING OR SUMMER. ALL OTHER TYPES—HORSE, COW, CHICKEN, AND SO ON—WHEN FRESH, CAN HARM PLANTS AND SHOULD BE COMPOSTED BEFORE APPLYING TO THE GARDEN. YOU CAN SPREAD FRESH MANURE OVER THE GARDEN AND TILL IT IN IMMEDIATELY, BUT YOU SHOULD WAIT FOUR WEEKS BEFORE PLANTING.

"MANURE TEA" CAN BE USED TO FERTILIZE HOUSEPLANTS AS WELL AS GARDEN PLANTS. TO "BREW" IT, STIR ONE PART MANURE INTO THREE PARTS WATER; LET IT SIT UNTIL IT IS THE COLOR OF TEA. USE THE TEA TO GIVE PLANTS A BOOST WHEN THEY ARE READY TO BLOOM. THE TEA IS ALSO GREAT FOR GET-TING TRANSPLANTS OFF TO A GOOD START.

The Right Tool

May God bless you with his special favor
and wonderful peace as you come to know
Jesus, our God and Lord, better and better.
As we know Jesus better, his divine power
gives us everything we need for living a godly
life. He has called us to receive his own glory
and goodness!

2 PETER 1:2-3

Garden tools haven't changed much over the centuries. Tools and equipment used in seventeenth-century gardens would look right at home in a twentieth-century garden shed.

None of my garden tools date back to 1600, but many are old and most were handed down to me. Some came from my parents, from whom I also inherited my gardening genes. Some of my tools belonged to a gardener who died at the age of 103! A few more came from a friend's uncle who had gardened well past his eightieth birthday.

I like these old, experienced tools. After thirty to fifty years of use, they have proven their mettle. And I think the "oldness" of them fits in with my idea of a garden: an established place, one that has taken shape and acquired character through the years.

You'll also find some things in my tool collection that look insignificant but are dear to me: several pairs of sticks wound with string, which I use to make straight rows for vegetables; a collection of nice labels and a permanent marker; stacks of pots of all sizes, both clay and plastic; and an old vegetable strainer that I use to sift soil. Years ago I found a small kitchen fork in the dirt near our house. I use it to gently pry apart tiny seedlings that have grown together in trays in the greenhouse. All of my tools are tried and true. They fit my hands, my budget, and my gardening style.

In my years as a follower of Jesus, I have found some "tried and true" tools that have kept me growing spiritually.

The year that I accepted Christ's invitation to receive his forgiveness and become his follower, I discovered Scripture memory. I was given a little booklet that told me how to memorize the Bible and why that was important. Memorizing God's Word became an effective tool for growth in my new life as a Christian. God's Word stored in my heart and mind was available to remind me of God's thoughts when I was tempted to think and behave in a way that didn't honor him. The verses I memorized helped me to refute Satan's attempts to discredit my faith in Christ. When friends had questions of a spiritual nature, I knew a few verses to share that we could discuss. I liked this tool. It was one Jesus had used himself.

Another tool that helps me grow as a Christian is Bible study. I still use several methods of digging into the Bible that I learned from more experienced Christians many years ago. As I study the Word of God, I continue to uncover treasures that are shaping my life.

Christians down through the ages have used many other tools to cultivate their spiritual growth, tools such as prayer, fasting, silence and solitude, and journaling. These tools, called "spiritual disciplines," have this purpose: to help us get to know Jesus better and follow him more closely. We put ourselves in a place of submission and openness to the Holy Spirit through the practice of spiritual disciplines.

I have tested my inherited garden tools and kept the ones that help me grow my garden. My test for the spiritual disciplines I follow is similar: Will this habit or method draw me closer to Christ? Will it help me to grow in godliness? As I continue to do those things that keep me growing spiritually, I can "come to know Jesus, our God and Lord, better and better." ❖

DIGGING DEEPER

The spiritual disciplines are not the habits of the grimly determined. Jesus was the most disciplined of all men, but his life was full of joy and passion. What spiritual tool or discipline will you include in your life so that you may get to know Jesus better and follow him more closely? What tools are you using already?

PRAYER

Lord, show me how to glean from the lives of experienced and wise Christians those tools that I need in my own life. Help me to be disciplined so that I might learn more of you.

GARDENING TIPS

CHEAP TOOLS ARE NEVER A BARGAIN. WELL-MADE TOOLS CAN BE EXPENSIVE, BUT THEY WILL ALWAYS DO THEIR JOB WELL AND LAST LONG ENOUGH FOR YOUR GRANDCHILDREN TO INHERIT THEM.

TRY A DIBBER OR DIBBLE. THIS WOODEN TOOL IS A TAPERED, SHARPLY POINTED STICK, SOMETIMES WITH A METAL CAP ON THE POINTED END, USED TO MAKE HOLES FOR PLANTING. YOU CAN MAKE A SMALL HOLE BY PUSHING ITS POINT IN THE SOIL A FRACTION (FOR TINY TRANSPLANTS), OR YOU CAN MAKE HOLES BIG ENOUGH TO PUT A BULB INTO. JUST POKE IT INTO THE GROUND AND ROTATE IT UNTIL THE HOLE IS THE SIZE YOU WANT. AFTER YOU PUT THE PLANT IN THE HOLE, POKE THE DIBBER IN THE SOIL IN A RING ALL AROUND THE PLANT. THIS ACTION PUSHES THE SOIL GENTLY AGAINST THE ROOTS OF THE PLANT, SO THEY MAKE GOOD CONTACT WITH THE SOIL.

43

Weeding and Praying

*[Daniel] continued kneeling on his
knees three times a day, praying and
giving thanks before his God.*

DANIEL 6:10, NASB

The summer that our youngest daughter got married, I spent a lot of
time on my knees. She and her husband-to-be wanted a garden wedding
reception, so I had major work to do, especially to get Blessing Hill ready
for the celebration.

Rudyard Kipling wrote that half a proper gardener's work is done on
his knees. A large part of this lowly work is due to weeds. The advent of
weeds dates back to the Fall.

After Adam's disobedience, God declared the ground to be cursed. "It
will grow thorns and thistles for you, though you will eat of its grains,"
God had said (Gen. 3:18). Because of this, weeds and other less-prized
plants are so tenacious and efficient that they keep cropping up everywhere. They use up the nutrients, space, and sunlight that the "good"
plants need. So every good gardener spends a lot of time weeding.

Weeding is a humble and personal chore. You have to get down close

44

to the earth so you can see to pull the weed out by the roots. Or you may need to untangle the weed from a plant you want to save. As you do the tedious pulling, you can also check on your garden's condition, the health of plants, the arrival of seedlings. Your face is right there close, so you can see into blossoms and smell the fragrances.

If you hand-weed your garden, you know what's in it. You learn by experience which seedling will become a weed and which is a stray marigold seedling come to live with the lilies. Still, many people use herbicides on their gardens to speed up the weeding chore. These poisons are fast, but they can harm the good plants nearby, too. And why hurry and miss the pleasantness of being surrounded by green life? The garden is one place where time seems stilled, where you can be relaxed even as you work.

Just as weeding keeps us involved and "intimate" with our gardens, praying maintains our personal relationship with the Lord. We bend our knees and bow our heart, and God allows us to grow in intimacy with him.

His holiness and love draw us to him in humility, worship, and surrender. He puts his hand on our life, touches those "weeds" that hinder growth—outright sin or just encumbrances—and instructs us to "weed" them out. We confess, repent, and ask for help, and the Lord assures us of his strength to maintain our newly "weeded heart."

When we know that we are forgiven and loved, we are at ease as we pray. God invites us to enjoy the pleasure of his company. With the Word of God as our guide, we learn how and what to pray. We may tell him whatever is on our mind, ask questions, or bring requests and needs, great or small. And he loves to say yes to us. I started a list once of all

my prayers that God has said yes to. The long list keeps growing.

And the weeds keep growing, too, so I am often out in the garden, kneeling as I weed, which is also the ideal posture for prayer. ✤

DIGGING DEEPER

What do you think about when you are weeding? When is the ideal time for you to spend time with God? Why not consider the garden as a place of prayer and turn your weeding time into prayer time?

PRAYER

Thank you, Father, for the privilege of prayer, that I may become intimate with you, the Holy One, the Creator of the universe. Teach me to pray. Thank you for the example of Daniel, who prayed so humbly and faithfully. And thank you for hearing and answering my prayers.

GARDENING TIPS

YOU CAN USE MULCH TO HELP FIGHT WEEDS. MULCH DEPRIVES WEED SEEDS OF SUNLIGHT. AS MULCHES DECOMPOSE, THEY ADD TO THE ORGANIC CONTENT OF THE SOIL.

SOME MULCHES TO USE: WOOD CHIPS, WOOD SHAVINGS, CRUSHED DRIED LEAVES, OLD STRAW. COMPOST, MANURE, PEAT MOSS, AND GROUND CORNCOB MULCHES SHOULD BE KEPT BACK A FEW INCHES FROM THE BASE OF PERENNIAL PLANTS. THESE MULCHES ARE HEAVY AND RETAIN SO MUCH MOISTURE THAT A FUNGUS COULD FORM AND ROT THE CROWN OR BASE OF THE PLANTS. SEVERAL LAYERS OF NEWSPAPER WORK WELL AS A MULCH BETWEEN CROP ROWS, ALTHOUGH THEY AREN'T PRETTY!

YOU CAN BUY WOOD CHIPS AND COCOA HULLS (FOR A GARDEN THAT SMELLS LIKE CHOCOLATE) AT A GARDEN STORE IF YOU HAVE THE MONEY TO SPEND. YOU CAN ALSO ASK YOUR FRIENDS TO SAVE THEIR RAKED LEAVES IN BAGS FOR YOU.

Pests: Who Invited You?

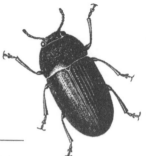

You will keep in perfect peace all who trust in you, whose thoughts are fixed on you!

ISAIAH 26:3

One afternoon I watched a chipmunk make quick work of a few dozen crickets. The crickets live in and around the stone wall on our terrace, where I was sitting. The chipmunk was flushing them out and munching them as fast as he could. I was glad for the chipmunk's windfall because crickets can do damage to a garden, especially to tender seedlings.

On another day I discovered a hickory horned devil on the ground near the chicken coop. This five-inch-long, fat, and fierce-looking caterpillar (the larvae of the royal walnut moth) is neon green, with dreadful orange and black spines. It had apparently fallen out of the hickory tree under which I was standing. I took its picture and tried to admire it.

Every garden has its insects, many of which can become pests. Flies and chewing worms, hordes of slugs, bean beetles, and such all cause trouble and sometimes despair for the gardener. Of course, if it weren't

48

for certain insects, we wouldn't have honey or seeds or fruit. We'd have no cotton, no silk. Nevertheless, too many bugs in the garden can be annoying and must be reckoned with.

Sometimes our thought life is full of "pests" also, especially when we try to pray. Like a cloud of gnats, doubts and worries or other distractions fill our mind. We wonder if we are feeling "spiritual" enough to pray. We have thoughts of self-accusation or self-doubt. Sometimes a to-do list makes itself important when we decide to spend time with God. If we were doing anything else, the list would not assert itself, but when we go to prayer, all other duties seem to loom. Our thoughts, like butterflies, flit from one distraction to another, disturbing our concentration and enjoyment of God's presence.

Keeping our mind focused on the Lord in prayer can be difficult because we can't see God. We often don't know what to say, what to ask for, or how to listen. Because of this, the temptation to skip prayer looms over us. But this is a battle that can be won. Here are some suggestions that may help: Reading a psalm out loud may keep our mind from wandering. Singing psalms and songs of praise to the Lord can heighten our sense of his nearness.

When doubts surface in prayer, we can ask the Lord for his peace. We

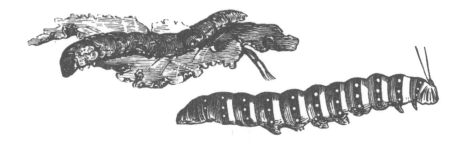

needn't pretend that we aren't fearful or that we don't have questions. We can let his character and his Word assure us of his hand on our life.

If we keep a notebook handy, we can jot down the distractions that come to mind. Pinning them down on paper can help free our mind to continue in prayer. Some of the thoughts that come may actually be ideas from God. We can write them down and pray about them later.

The physical act of kneeling as we pray keeps us aware that we are in the presence of Almighty God.

The garden will always have its six- and eight-legged inhabitants. Some we will have to get rid of. We can learn to tolerate and even appreciate others. As for those pesky thoughts that regularly interrupt our prayers, we can pray for patience with our own weaknesses. And we can ask God to teach us how to be still and at peace in his presence. ✢

DIGGING DEEPER

When is your concentration in prayer most difficult? What distractions or thoughts keep you from enjoying your time with God? Perhaps a change in time and place for prayer could minimize the distractions and renew your joy and peace as you meet with the Lord.

PRAYER

Whenever I am distracted, please quiet my frenetic thoughts, Lord, and give me your peace. Help me, Holy One, to fix my thoughts on you so that I may be truly present in your presence.

GARDENING TIPS

IF YOU'RE BUGGED BY BUGS, TRY ENTICING BIRDS TO PATROL YOUR GARDEN FOR INSECTS. THE BIRDS MAY EAT SOME OF YOUR FRUIT AND ORNAMENTAL BERRIES, BUT THEY ARE STRONG ALLIES AGAINST INSECT PESTS. JUST PROVIDE WATER, NESTING BOXES, AND FOOD, AND THEY'LL EAT AS MUCH AS FOUR TIMES THEIR WEIGHT IN INSECTS EACH DAY.

IN THE MEANTIME, APHIDS ON ROSES AND OTHER PLANTS AND FLOWERS CAN BE CONTROLLED BY SPRAYING THE PLANTS FORCE-FULLY WITH THE GARDEN HOSE EVERY FEW DAYS.

SOME PESTS HAVE TO BE HANDPICKED FROM YOUR PLANTS. CARRY A CAN OF KEROSENE AROUND IN THE GARDEN AND KNOCK JAPANESE BEETLES, CABBAGE CATERPILLARS, AND POTATO BEETLES INTO THE CAN. AFTERWARD, PUT A LID ON THE CAN AND DISPOSE.

WANT MORE BIRDS IN YOUR BACKYARD? PLANT PURPLE CONE FLOWERS, SUNFLOWERS, CRAB APPLE TREES, AND ANY KIND OF BERRIES. HUMMINGBIRDS LOVE TRUMPET-SHAPED FLOW-ERS, ESPECIALLY RED ONES.

Less Is More

*I am the true vine, and my Father is the
gardener. He cuts off every branch that doesn't
produce fruit, and he prunes the branches that
do bear fruit so they will produce even more. . . .
Yes, I am the vine; you are the branches.*

JOHN 15:1-2, 5

A just-pruned grapevine can be an alarming sight. As much as 90 percent or more of the vine has to be removed if it hasn't been pruned for a few years. How can such harsh treatment be helpful? Ask the owner of the vine a year later. He'll show you lots of high-quality fruit that he never would have harvested before the drastic pruning job.

Many cultivated plants need a controlling hand to help them become their best. For instance, the roses along our driveway send long arching canes over the road, so I have to cut them back and train them to take another direction by tying them to the fence regularly. If I didn't do this, the canes would become rank, sparsely flowered, and a nuisance. The result of the severe cutting back of those canes is a fence full of roses in spring.

Privet *(Ligustrum vulgare)* is another plant that needs a firm hand. We planted a privet hedge around the *potager* and trained it to form an arch over the entry gate. Privet grows fast and loose, so several times a season my husband has to get tough with it. He prunes and shapes, molding the hedge to his liking. All this pruning has caused the privet to thicken into a handsome shape.

Plants that take to pruning become more than they were, better than they could be if left alone.

Since we are the branches attached to Jesus the vine, we can expect God, the faithful and wise gardener, to do some pruning in our life. He prunes so that we can become all that Christ saved us for and wants us to be.

He will point out anything that hinders our growth in Christ. This can be uncomfortable at times. He may ask us to take pruning shears and trim away little things like pastimes that keep us from the Word and prayer or habits that eat away at our confidence in Christ.

When God does the pruning himself, he sometimes uses drastic measures. He may allow setbacks, disappointments, or failures in order to enlarge our capacity to hear him and become even more fruitful. He loves us enough to allow us to be hurt at times but never harms us. We can be sure his pruning is always governed by his tenderness and love for us, even though the pruning process is sometimes very painful. His kind hands take hold of our life and shape it, making it into a vessel that glorifies him.

We can't "grow" properly on our own, just as a garden can't remain healthy without tender care. On our own, we gradually become less than God intended in his good will for us. But as we submit to his bending and breaking and pruning, Christ's character will be formed in us.

When God does some pruning in our life, he has one thing in mind: our fruit-bearing capacity. This fruit is the increase of Christlikeness in us. God's pruning is always merciful, always leading to more abundant life. ✤

DIGGING DEEPER

Has the Holy Spirit shown you something in your life that needs to be pruned away? Or are you in the middle of a pruning time and feeling more pain than progress? Trust the Lord to do a perfect job of healing the wound. In his time, you will see more blossoms and fruit in your life than you ever thought possible.

PRAYER

Father, we would be afraid to surrender to the pruning knife of anyone else but you. Thank you for the pruning that draws us closer to you and helps us to become more like your Son.

Gardening Tips

The basics of pruning are these: cut off any dead, broken, or diseased branches as well as any growth that is a structural defect. If you know how the tree or shrub should look when fully developed, you can cut away anything that hinders a strong growth pattern and symmetry. Cuts must be made clean, not ragged or ripped, so use sharp tools. You'll need to cut back to a growth point—a bud—when you prune. This diverts energy back to other buds on the branch, and new growth pops out with vigor.

Knowing the growth habits of your plants, trees, and shrubs is important if you want to prune properly. Consult a gardening encyclopedia or the many books in the library that refer to specific plants. This is especially important when you want to prune in order to increase the output of fruit trees.

Life in a Garden

Not even a sparrow, worth only half a penny,
can fall to the ground without your Father
knowing it. And the very hairs on your head are
all numbered. So don't be afraid; you are more
valuable to him than a whole flock of sparrows.

MATTHEW 10:29-31

I have come outside to sit on the terrace and read, but the life in my garden distracts me. A butterfly lands on my chair cushion just under my elbow. It's a white cabbage butterfly with two black splotches on each wing. I shouldn't like this creature. Its eggs hatch into bright green caterpillars that eat holes in my cabbage and kale. But here it is, so near and seemingly precious. I see its eyes up close and wonder, *What does it see of me?*

The butterfly soon leaves my chair, then returns and tries to land on my hand. I continue to take in the color of life around me, ignoring my book. There's a goldfinch eating seeds from a thistle I neglected to pull out of the flower bed. I see purple petunias and red verbena. A pumpkin vine with dark green leaves like satellite dishes is growing along the top of the privet hedge. Rusty red chrysanthemums are in bud. A tiger swal-

56

lowtail butterfly is sipping from a pale violet phlox. Suddenly, the swallowtail flies up to me, right into my face, then flits away.

All this life in my garden and everywhere else on our planet belongs to the Father in heaven. Whether a bird or butterfly or people in the plane overhead, all living things are under his absolute supervision.

This is one of the implications of Jesus' words about the sparrow falling. God knows, God sees what happens to his creatures. Also, Jesus said that a person is worth more to God than a whole flock of sparrows, even though he takes note of the death of every tiny bird.

God is alert to everything that is going on in and around us. He monitors the life that flows through the cells in our hair follicles. He keeps a tally of the hair growth and fallout from each head.

Why should God want to know these things? Because, Jesus says, God loves us. We are precious to him, so precious that he knows the smallest details of our body and our mind. The Lord God, the fountain of life, has revealed himself to us in Jesus Christ because he wants us to know his love.

God's love for us is so great that nothing can touch us without first passing through the filter of his love. Jesus wants this truth to fill us with confidence. We need not fear anything or anyone on earth. We need only fear God. We are to reverence him, acknowledge his greatness, and his great love for us. When Jesus was here on earth, he often said to people, "Don't be afraid" (Luke 12:32; John 14:27). He said this in the direst situations, even in the face of death.

Don't be afraid. These words are the essence of the good news of Jesus Christ, and they are scattered throughout the pages of the Bible. See, for example, Joshua 1:9. God wants us to feel secure, so he tells us repeatedly, "I love you. Don't be afraid."

We have hung some bird bottles under the eaves of our house. Sparrows are the uncontested residents of these bottles every spring. They are just ordinary, noisy house sparrows. But because of what Jesus has said about sparrows, they have become a symbol of God's love for me. Their little ordinary lives remind me every day that I have nothing to fear because God is keeping his eye on me. All is well. ❖

DIGGING DEEPER

Is it hard for you to believe that you are valuable to God? Why or why not? You might set a goal to read the Gospel of John and take note of how often God's love for you is mentioned. Listen to him as he says, "I love you. I died for you. I live for you. Don't be afraid."

PRAYER

My Lord and my God, I am in awe of your creation and your love for me. Thank you for my life. Give me a heart that yearns to recognize more of your intimate care for me.

Gardening Tips

If you want to attract butterflies to your garden, plant these flowers: zinnias, phlox, coreopsis, "Autumn Joy" sedum, cosmos, asclepias tuberosa (butterfly weed). Milkweed, dill, and fennel are favorite foods of butterfly larvae. Butterfly houses are for sale in garden catalogs and nurseries, but butterflies can fend for themselves in any garden where there are flowers, shrubs, and trees.

Butterflies also love buddleia, called appropriately "butterfly bush." This is a lovely shrub with purple, pink, or white clusters of fragrant flowers that bloom May through August, depending on the variety. Buddleia is easy to grow, blooming on growth of the current year. Some buddleia bushes can reach a height of fifteen feet in one season. You'll need to cut the vigorous branches back severely in the fall or early spring to encourage more branching and flower production.

Heaven

*Look, the home of God is now among his
people! He will live with them, and they will be
his people. God himself will be with them. He
will remove all of their sorrows, and there will be
no more death or sorrow or crying or pain. For
the old world and its evils are gone forever.*

REVELATION 21:3-4

In my garden I see lush, exuberant color everywhere I look. The yellow
gold coreopsis are blooming, adding more sunlight to an already bright
day. The large purple allium are gently swaying in the breeze. I can see
roses and coralbells and sedum's yellow star blooms.

Every summer surprises me with its freshness. Every year, I wonder:
*Have I really seen all this beauty before? Was the sun ever this bright, this
warm?* I feel as though I'll burst with joy because of the early days of
summer.

In the present reality of summertime, I try to picture the little water-
fall frozen, the trees bare, the grass brown, everything under cruel ice
and stillness. It's hard to keep that dead image in mind as I view the life

around me. But I know that summertime is a transient reality. It can be enjoyed and appreciated but not held on to, not in this hemisphere, not on this earth. I can let the summer sun warm my bones and my heart as I think of how summertime is a little bit like being in heaven. Heaven is the eternal reality.

Things in nature don't operate as God originally intended, however beautiful they appear from time to time. But one glorious day this earth and all its functions and malfunctions will cease. We will have pure summertime all the time. God and the Lamb will light up all things so there will be no more night and no need of a sun.

When hard things come into my life, when my heart feels frozen, I can remember what's coming. While we're on earth, God means for us to comfort ourselves with thoughts of the bright future in heaven. This is not so we can escape the present but so we may be strengthened until the trouble is over. This will be the glory of heaven: laughter and reveling in the eternal truth of Jesus' conquest of all pain and sin and death. We will experience that conquest, that deliverance, that joy, forever and ever.

Heaven will be . . . well . . . heavenly, because the reality of sorrow, and all its reasons, will have been redeemed and transformed. In heaven, God's own fingers will wipe all tears away. Then will come the great revelation: We will know the meaning of the details,

61

both painful and pleasant, of our existence. Then we will know as we are known. We will be surrounded by light, the greatness and holiness and love of God. All things will be made new.

I'm thankful for the rhythms of the earth, the beauty of the seasons. They are part of the plan until Jesus returns. God designed these rhythms with us in mind so that we would have both work and rest, the energy

that comes from the sun, and the quiet that falls with the snow. But summer is my favorite season because of what happens in my garden, and also because it reminds me of the eternal summer that is to come. ✢

DIGGING DEEPER

What do you most look forward to in your life here on earth? What do you look forward to when you think of being in heaven with God? When do thoughts of heaven provide you the most comfort?

PRAYER

My Lord and my God, you are so great. You have let me see in your Word a glimpse of eternity, of how it will be to always be with you. Thank you for your presence with me now in this day. Help me to keep my eyes on Jesus so that I may live in joyful anticipation of my heavenly home.

Gardening Tips

While there are some "rules" as to color arrangement in the garden (according to the many books on the subject), you don't have to let the rules override your preferences. Plant what you love! Many gardeners are rediscovering the "old-fashioned" flowers that are trouble-free and cheerful all summer long. Among these old-but-new flowers are: hollyhocks, dianthus, four-o'clocks, verbena, hydrangeas, lilies, phlox, and coreopsis.

If you cut the top few inches off phlox plants sometime during the last two weeks of June, the plants will send out multiple branches and give you more blossoms for a longer period. You can cut back the tops of all your plants, or just half of them, leaving the uncut ones to develop blossoms while the new shoots are forming on the cut plants.

Living Water

If there is one blessing missing from Blessing Hill, it's water. Of course,
we have running water in the house taps, supplied by the county. But
naturally occurring water—a stream or spring—is not one of my
garden's features. My husband and I tried to create the illusion of a little
stream by planting several hundred grape hyacinth bulbs in a shallow
gully in the woodland garden. I had seen this idea produce a brilliant
effect in a garden in Holland.

Our bulbs didn't perform with the same brilliance, mostly because the
squirrels dug many of them up and either ate them or replanted them
elsewhere. I found grape hyacinth growing in the vegetable garden and
in the rose bed. And so many leaves fell in the gully that the small bulbs
were eventually smothered.

I still yearn for a real stream or spring on our property. Running water is refreshing and soothing. It makes me thoughtful, giving me feelings of peace and joy all at once. Moving water gives the sense of an endless supply, the feeling that I could sit beside it forever and it would never be depleted.

Moving, running water, as in rivers, streams, and springs, is what the Israelites called "living water." Water that continues to bubble or flow does seem alive and imparts a feeling of life to the beholder or the drinker. Moving water is usually considered fresh, clean, and healthful.

The Feast of Tabernacles was a week-long celebration of noise and merrymaking when the Israelites remembered their wanderings in the wilderness. More sacrifices were offered at this feast than at any other. During the feast, they performed a ceremony each day called *Libatio aquae*—the pouring out of water. A golden bowl was used to fetch water from the pool of Siloam; this water was then poured out as an offering to the Lord, with shouts, trumpet fanfares, and expressions of joy.

When Jesus stood and called to the crowds on that last day of that joyous feast, he wanted the people to learn something new, to connect that pouring water with himself. So he said, "Are you thirsty? Come to me. I have living water for you." In one sense, he was saying, "Do you want real life and a joy that will be continuous? Come to me."

What Jesus offered then and now is not water fetched from a pool but living water, a continuous stream that will become part of our true self.

If we come to Christ, our life can become like a garden that has a constant supply of water. As Isaiah tells us, "The Lord will guide you continually, watering your life when you are dry and keeping you healthy, too. You will be like a well-watered garden, like an ever-flowing spring" (Isa. 58:11). The Holy Spirit indwelling us will refresh our souls every day and make our life fruitful and refreshing to others.

A friend took care of our garden while we were away for a week. This faithful friend watered so well that our garden was luxuriant while the rest of the county suffered through a drought. We came home to abundant fruit and flowers. Our friend's diligent care produced a perfect picture of what the Lord does for thirsty people who come to him for living water. ❖

DIGGING DEEPER

What are the things you've tried that you thought would satisfy but which left you feeling disappointed? What does it mean to you that Jesus offers you living water? How have you experienced that living water in your life? What would you like to tell others of Jesus' offer of living water?

PRAYER

Lord, you said I would never thirst again if I received your gift of living water. But I do thirst for more of you, to know you better, to sense more of your presence in my life. I'm thankful that I can always come to you for a drink because the supply is eternal. Daily you quench my thirst as I come to you for forgiveness, companionship, and guidance.

Gardening Tips

WATERING BY HAND IN THE EVENING IS A GOOD PRACTICE. THE WATER SOAKS IN WITHOUT EVAPORATING AS QUICKLY AS IT WOULD DURING THE HEAT OF DAY. IF YOU ELECT TO USE SPRINKLERS, HOWEVER, THE EARLY MORNING IS BEST FOR WATERING YOUR GARDEN. THIS ALLOWS THE PLANTS TO DRY OFF.

KEEP A BUCKET OF WATER HANDY WHEN YOU ARE HARVESTING CARROTS, BEETS, AND OTHER ROOT CROPS. AFTER YOU RINSE THE DIRT OFF THESE VEGETABLES IN THE BUCKET, YOU CAN SPRINKLE THE WATER ON THE THIRSTY PLANTS. THIS KEEPS THE SOIL IN THE GARDEN AND OUT OF YOUR KITCHEN.

HOUSEPLANTS NEED AN OCCASIONAL RINSING TO REMOVE DUST AND KEEP THE LEAVES HEALTHY. PUT ALL YOUR HOUSEPLANTS IN THE TUB AND TURN THE SHOWER ON THEM.

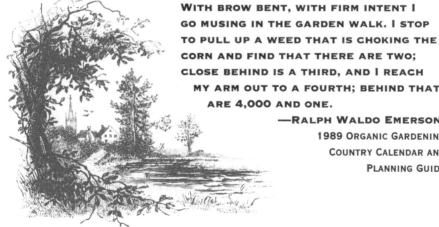

WITH BROW BENT, WITH FIRM INTENT I GO MUSING IN THE GARDEN WALK. I STOP TO PULL UP A WEED THAT IS CHOKING THE CORN AND FIND THAT THERE ARE TWO; CLOSE BEHIND IS A THIRD, AND I REACH MY ARM OUT TO A FOURTH; BEHIND THAT ARE 4,000 AND ONE.

—RALPH WALDO EMERSON,
1989 ORGANIC GARDENING
COUNTRY CALENDAR AND
PLANNING GUIDE

67

AUTUMN
The Garden Gives Gifts

I think fall is my favorite time especially this fall, when the clear days and frostless nights seem to go on forever, and the sweet-olive gives out a fragrance that is like a farewell to summer. The summer flowers have faded, and their spent stalks have been cleared away, but the new buds unfurl as petals fall, and one door opens as another shuts.

Elizabeth Lawrence

A Walk in the Woods

The path of the righteous is like the first gleam
of dawn, shining ever brighter till the full light
of day.

PROVERBS 4:18, NIV

What would you do with a roof tile from a sixteenth-century Scottish church? I have such a tile, and it looks like it will last another four hundred years. I painted the word *Woodswalk* on it and propped it up against a rock at the east corner of our hilltop. This tile sign is meant to be an invitation to venture in among the trees and take a stroll through my small woodland garden. This is where I let things go as they grow, hoping to keep the "Woodswalk" natural looking.

I knew when our family first moved here that, whatever else I did, I would make a path through the little woods. I wanted to walk among the trees and find delights as I went. I wanted the path to look orderly enough that visitors would be enticed to take a stroll and make their own discoveries.

The Woodswalk began as a path of least resistance. For one thing, there were some large oaks and a cluster of maples that I couldn't move. There

were also some dips and rises in the terrain that I
wanted to use. During our second summer on Blessing Hill, I wove my way through the brush, clippers
in hand, snipping saplings, brambles, and branches,
reorganizing but not conquering, making mental
notes of what was growing where. I found a crowd
of jack-in-the-pulpits and knew the path had to go
near but not over that spot. Gradually the path took
shape and direction. I lined part of the path with
hosta when someone gave me a boxful. We bought
twenty-five very small rhododendrons and scattered
them throughout the woods. My brother gave me ten
azaleas. Into the woods they all went.

I wanted people to see the path and think, *I'll
follow it and see where it leads.* And I wanted it to be
wide enough for two to walk side by side comfortably. The path developed into a winding trail, moving
into and out of shadows, taking the walker on a mini-expedition
of mid-Atlantic nature.

Two small children took a walk through my woods with me one
summer day. They were city kids, and the little woodland seemed huge
to them. They began to feel lost and then afraid and wanted to see their
mother. Their perspective of my Woodswalk was so different from mine,
because I have walked the path before.

God's plan for our life is like my woodland path. It moves us along
little by little, taking us on an adventure, a discovery of beauty and truth

and of the Father's intimate care for us. His path is designed to keep us close to him, and we discover his love for us at every turn.

Walking along God's planned path, we may meet obstacles. We may become frightened, like the children were along my woodland path. Yet

God promises to help us find a way around the obstacles or through them. He knows our path because he saw it before we took our first steps. When the way seems obscure, he sows light like seed, scattering it ahead of our feet, enough light to move forward even if it is but a step. Just as the sun comes up and gradually fills the day with light, so God makes his will for his children clear by small and steady degrees.

God's plans for our life, like a garden path, reveal more and more beauty with each step we take. As we continue walking in obedience to him, God helps us along to maturity in Christ. ✣

DIGGING DEEPER

You are blessed, which means "on the right path," if you belong to Christ. What is there about your life path that gives you joy? What, if anything, makes you uneasy? Trust the Lord to restore your confidence in his presence and guidance in your life.

PRAYER

Dear God, I thank you that you have given me the righteousness of your Son and have put my feet on your path. Thank you that you are my Light and my Guide as I continue along, following Jesus.

Gardening Tips

Whether you are making walkways between your vegetables, or paths along flower beds, consider these points:

Width. If the path is in the vegetable garden, it needs to be wide enough to accommodate a tiller or a wheelbarrow; a path that leads along flower beds and vistas ought to be wide enough in most places for two to walk comfortably side by side.

Material. Bricks make durable and beautiful paths. If set in the ground on edge, it is easier to make attractive patterns with them, but this process uses up more bricks. Large slabs of slate are attractive; their color blends well with flowers and foliage. Pine bark and wood chips are perfect for a shade garden or a woods walk. Whatever material you use, your aim should be to make the path as beautiful as possible, easy to maintain, and a complement to the loveliness of your garden.

73

Death of a Cherry Tree

May the Lord of peace himself always give you
his peace no matter what happens.

2 THESSALONIANS 3:16

The demise of our cherry tree wasn't caused by someone with a hatchet. It just died—not from old age, not from any obvious disease. One spring it produced flowers, then cherries. Then one day all the cherries started to rot on the tree, and the leaves fell after that. The tree was dead. In just a few days it was obvious that there was no life in any of the branches. What happened?

My husband didn't want to believe the tree had died. He waited until the following spring, hoping to see some green on it somewhere. He finally cut it down and looked at a cross section of the trunk. There was no rotten core—just beautiful cherry wood.

The cherry tree was one of many trees on the northern slope of our hill. We call this group of trees our "orchard," even though that word is a bit too grand for it. The orchard is also where I have a small plot of wildflowers that I call my "meadow." It's the tiniest meadow you'll ever see, but I wanted to have a place to let wildflowers grow freely. They never look quite at home in the more formal flower beds.

The other trees in the orchard and the flowers in the meadow were healthy and lovely. Why then did the cherry tree die?

Every one of us lives with some unsolved mystery. And while the Word of God is full of answers to the many knotty problems of life, there will still be some things that we will never understand fully. Of course, the overnight loss of a healthy, mature, and beautiful cherry tree does not have the same weight of grief and questioning attached as the unexpected loss of a job or the sudden death of a loved one. In those heavy times, when we feel blindsided, our *why* is a pain that is magnified by the silence of God. How can we find peace when we don't have answers?

Often God keeps us in suspense. He asks us to trust him and live with questions and puzzles. We may seek God for answers and are encouraged, in fact, to do so. He tells us to pray about everything, to seek and expect an answer (see Matt. 7:7-8). Our spirit is lifted when we hear an answer to the questions in our heavy heart.

But sometimes this formula doesn't seem to work. That's when we discover that God wants to give us *himself,* rather than an answer to our *why.* His love cultivates trust in our heart as he provides his marvelous peace "no matter what happens" (2 Thess. 3:16). So we pour out our questions, fears, and hurts. Since nothing takes God by surprise and no question stumps him, we can rest in his wise and loving ordering of our life. We can begin to release our grip on our need for answers.

The mystery of the cherry tree may be solved. I have just read about a disease called *verticillium wilt* that kills trees fast. Alas, there is no cure for it; but my husband has written a happy ending to this story. He's going to make a piece of furniture from the cherry wood.

We will have other unfinished stories and heavier questions to carry to heaven, where God has all the answers. And he is all we really need today. He is our peace as we trust him to give us his love, comfort, help, and, eventually, the answers we seek. ❖

DIGGING DEEPER

Do you have an unsolved mystery that keeps you from experiencing the peace of God? What is it about this unsolved mystery that the Lord might be teaching you? Have you sought the God of all answers as well as the answer itself? What can you do to release your struggle to the Lord?

PRAYER

I long to love you, Lord, not only for all that you do for me but for yourself. Help me to not let my questions get in the way of my worship and rob me of a quiet heart. Thank you for the peace that comes when I acknowledge your sovereignty in my life and surrender my questions to you.

Gardening Tips

A dwarf fruit tree can be a lovely focal point in your vegetable garden. Since it will not block sunlight from your crops, you can put it in the middle of the garden and plant some herbs at its feet. Dwarf fruit trees bear the same size fruit as standard-size trees. A "bonanza" peach is a good choice. Its shiny leaves and tight growth habit are a pleasing contrast to the loose growth of herbs like oregano and thyme.

A part of your lawn may be turned into a meadow. Wildflowers need sun, so choose a sunny spot and cover it with black plastic in the summer or fall. Come spring, remove the plastic, and plow or spade under the dead grass. Rake the area smooth, and scatter wildflower seeds that are native to your area. Keep the soil moist for several weeks until the seedlings are a few inches high.

Have Some More

God will generously provide all you
need. Then you will always have everything you
need and plenty left over to share with others.

2 CORINTHIANS 9:8

Every time I see the rose campion in the perennial bed or the epimedium in the woodland garden, I think of Mr. and Mrs. Thomas. My husband and I were once invited to stop in at their home while we traveled through Pennsylvania, though we had never met them. (They are the parents of a friend.)

When we pulled into their drive, I knew we had arrived at the home of kindred spirits. The Thomas house sits in the middle of a beautifully kept garden filled with plants that were new to me. As we chatted and walked around in the garden, I began to comment on certain plants I didn't recognize. By the time we were ready to continue our journey home, our new friends had filled up two large boxes with plants for our Maryland garden.

Gardeners are a generous lot. You rarely leave them empty-handed. They love to give away extra plants, a bouquet, or garden-grown produce. They freely share their knowledge with anyone just starting a garden.

Henry Mitchell, the garden writer, pointed out that gardeners *do* hate to part with a few things, like dirt, clay pots, good labels, stakes, twine, or any kind of wooden box. But other than these peculiar treasures, gardeners are always pleased to give away some of the glory of their gardens.

We always have something to share if we have a garden. Sometimes I like to think about where some of my garden offspring now live. A maple tree that was born on our hill grows in Colorado. Cleome, Virginia bluebells, and nicotiana have moved from my garden to several other states. My garden makes me feel rich because I can pass on what it produces to others.

If we are children of God, we always have something to share, too. God doesn't use a meager measure when he gives to us. He is a generous God who loves to be extravagant with us, so we can be generous like him.

God may sometimes be lavish in providing material things. When Jesus performed the miracle at the wedding in Cana (John 2), he was not skimpy with his solution to the problem of no more wine. Jesus made more than 120 gallons of wine for that wedding party!

Most often we experience God's liberality in spiritual blessings that come to us daily. His very presence with us, his Word that speaks to our heart, his help in temptation—these are gifts to us that we may share with those around us who need encouragement.

God has given us freely of his Spirit, who leads us, counsels us, and gives us joy. The fruit of the Spirit grows in us so that we may give ourselves away to those who are hungry for a glimpse of God.

When we are generous with what we have, not just from our gardens, but with other things in our life—like our time, our money, our possessions, our love—we show that we trust God to meet our needs. This kind of extravagant giving honors the Lord. Our generosity makes it possible for others to praise him, too. When we share with others, we become channels through which God may give gifts to others.

Everywhere I look on Blessing Hill, I see evidence of the love and generosity of others. The look of my garden has changed over the years because of the gifts of generous gardeners. I like what I see. ❖

DIGGING DEEPER

Perhaps you cannot see any evidence of God's generous hand in your life right now. If so, you might feel needy rather than in a position to be generous. Ask the Lord to open your eyes to what he has done for you. Trust God and believe that he will meet all of your needs, just as he promised. Read Ephesians 1–2, to encourage your heart.

PRAYER

Lord God, thank you for all that I have in my Savior, Jesus. Thank you for choosing me to be a part of your family. Make me a generous giver like you. Make me alert to opportunities where I can give to others as you have given to me.

Gardening Tips

If possible, plant a row of flowers just for cutting and giving away. Then pot your extra plants so they'll be ready to give away. Use orange juice cans, egg cartons, or any small containers. You might take your garden's gifts to church, to a friend's house, or to a homeless shelter or food bank.

Celebrate the beauty of your garden by sharing it with someone. Invite some friends or neighbors over or cook something for them that you grew in your garden.

Many herbs are still green in the autumn garden. You might enclose a sprig of feverfew, sage, or thyme in letters to friends.

Sowing Seeds

My true disciples produce much fruit. This
brings great glory to my Father. . . . I appointed
you to go and produce fruit that will last.

JOHN 15:8, 16

We've made an arch of privet over the entry gate to the *potager*. We chose privet *(Ligustrum vulgare)* because it chose us. There were privet seedlings and privet shrubs all over our hill. It was an economical decision to dig them up and use them for a hedge first and then for the arch. We keep the hedge around the *potager* trimmed to a height of four feet, so it doesn't usually bloom. The arch is now tall enough to produce small white fragrant flowers. The flowers become dark blue-black berries, which birds like to eat.

Some garden writers I have read cast scorn on the lowly privet. Too commonplace, they say, too uninteresting, too old-fashioned, not very satisfactory. Well, be that as it may, privet chose us, as I said before. It seeds itself so willingly and thrives here on Blessing Hill, so I guess that makes it commonplace. But privet has proven very satisfactory for our garden. In mild winters, it remains in a semi-evergreen state. And even though it is a vigorous grower, it has been easy to train into the hedge and arch we wanted. And because privet has the habit of making thousands more like itself, I don't think I'll ever run out of hedge material.

God wants us to be like privet. We are to be prolific seed bearers and seed casters, like the sower Jesus described in the parable of the sower (Mark 4). Through us, the good news of Jesus Christ can be spread around. Most of us are already a good deal like the privet in our garden, just ordinary, not spectacular, not greatly talented. But Jesus will multiply the life of an ordinary but faithful and willing disciple. We just have to give him what we have.

Jesus said that people will believe in him because of our testimony (John 17:20). Our testimony is our story of what Christ has done for us. Sharing our stories with someone can plant seeds of faith in that person's heart, too. Our life is also our testimony that supports what we say. Our deeds of kindness and thoughtfulness are seeds.

Fertile soil is hard to find in the hearts of people today. Our loving contact with people, our prayer, and patience are like a "cover crop" that is planted to protect and nourish the soil. The cover crop is plowed back into the soil so that when the main crop (the gospel) is planted, it will flourish.

Some of us will be seed sowers in the hearts of people. Some of us will get to carry the hose and watering can. Some of us will get to bring in the harvest. We work as a team in the body of Christ when it comes to planting the seed of the Word of God.

A seed's growth may be hindered. Satan snatches God's Word out of the hearts of some listeners. Other people happily believe until problems come. Sometimes God's message is crowded out by cares and desires.

Since so much can happen to seed to keep it from growing, God helps us to be prolific like privets, spreading God's Word around generously and skillfully. He has given us the privilege of coworking with him. When we share the good news of Christ with someone, whether by word or deed, God can make the seed sprout into life eternal. ✤

DIGGING DEEPER

How did you come to trust in Christ for your salvation? Consider writing it down as simply and briefly as possible, and ask the Lord to give you an opportunity to share it with a friend. Is there someone you can think of right now who needs to hear the gospel message?

PRAYER

Lord, I would love the privilege of introducing someone to you. Please help my words and life to speak clearly of you so that I may plant seeds of faith that you can make grow in _____'s life.
(Fill in the name of someone you've been praying for.)

GARDENING TIPS

MANY ANNUALS AND PERENNIALS ARE GENEROUS SELF-SOWERS.
ONCE YOU PLANT THEM IN YOUR GARDEN, YOU'LL ALWAYS HAVE
THEM AROUND. ALYSSUM, FEVERFEW, AGERATUM, JOHNNY-JUMP-
UPS, LUNERIA, VERBENA, CLEOME, AND MARIGOLDS ARE JUST A
FEW OF THE FLOWERS THAT PRODUCE LOTS OF SEED EACH YEAR.
YOU'LL FIND SEEDLINGS OF THESE FLOWERS IN SURPRISING PLACES.
THESE ARE CALLED "VOLUNTEERS." YOU MIGHT LEAVE THEM WHERE
THEY HAVE CHOSEN TO GROW OR TRANSPLANT THEM ACCORDING
TO YOUR GARDEN DESIGN. YOU CAN ALSO COLLECT THE SEED
BEFORE IT FALLS TO THE GROUND OR GETS "PLANTED" BY THE
BIRDS OR THE WIND.

CARRY A PLASTIC BAG OR
SMALL PLASTIC CONTAINER WITH
YOU IN YOUR TRAVELS AND
VISITS TO GARDENS. YOU MAY
COME ACROSS SOME PLANTS
GOING TO SEED THAT YOU COULD
BRING HOME TO TRY IN YOUR
OWN GARDEN.

The Garden Inside of Us

That is why we never give up. Though our bodies are dying, our spirits are being renewed every day. For our present troubles are quite small and won't last very long. Yet they produce for us an immeasurably great glory that will last forever!

2 CORINTHIANS 4:16-17

Autumn is the year's last hurrah. Fruit and seeds abound in the fall garden along with pumpkins, squash, asters, chrysanthemums, and even a few roses. The leaves on the trees are dying in splendor. Bright shimmering color is everywhere, as if the woods and garden are celebrating all that happened in them during the year.

Autumn becomes grave after the celebration. Not everything dies beautifully. The flower beds look forlorn with their ragged remains of summer's lushness. The first frost has turned many of the tender annuals into blackened mush. The days are shorter, less sunny. Melancholy slips into the autumn day as a chill comes into the air. The autumn chill invigorates but also makes me somber and introspective. The decreasing daylight reminds me that I cannot work in the garden much longer this season. And I think about the time that may come when I will not be able to work in the garden at all because of some infirmity.

The longer we live, the more likely we will experience "present troubles" that Paul speaks about in 2 Corinthians. These troubles may be due to the fact that our bodies are experiencing an autumn of sorts. Our pace slows, physical strength diminishes, and eyesight dims. We are forced to acknowledge that our earthly bodies are perishable.

Another kind of "trouble" we may have is due to living in this ruined world day after day. Difficulties may also come because we are in a hard place, on "assignment" from God. Someone has said that by middle age, we should be about half used up. When we allow God to "use us up," he may put us in places and situations where we might suffer.

A wonderful thing is happening to our spirit as our body undergoes physical changes due to age or circumstances. Our "inside life"—our soul, our inner self—is becoming more alive, more like a summer garden. This inner growth of beauty and strength and joy happens most often as a result of difficulties. While the outside of us is growing autumn-y, or just weary from struggle, we are actually getting stronger and brighter on the inside.

God knows all about any trouble we may be experiencing. He knows

that we sometimes feel as though we cannot bear the situation any longer. He feels our distress.

But, says God, the trouble is only temporary. Trust in my good purpose and constant presence with you. I am forming the life of Jesus in you. And you must believe this: Compared to what I have planned for you in heaven, what you have to endure here on earth is minor and brief.

The psalmist gives us further encouragement as he writes, "The godly

will flourish like palm trees and grow strong like the cedars of Lebanon. For they are transplanted into the Lord's own house. They flourish in the courts of our God. Even in old age they will still produce fruit; they will remain vital and green" (Ps. 92:12-14).

We can take comfort in the fact that the hard things in our life are making us more like Christ and are getting the insides of us ready to be joined to a totally new and eternal body. And God intends for us to live life with him to the fullest, no matter what our age. We are not dying like the autumn garden. We are flourishing like a well-kept garden in "the Lord's own house." ❖

DIGGING DEEPER

What do you look forward to doing as you grow older? How do you feel about this new stage of your life? What good things have you seen God bring out of the bad circumstances that have happened in your life?

PRAYER

Father, thank you for the promises you have given that encourage me when I am struggling and weary. Teach me to endure and rejoice because you are creating in me a beautiful garden that will bring praise and glory to you.

GARDENING TIPS

LOOKING FOR WAYS TO DECORATE YOUR THANKSGIVING TABLE? PRESS BRIGHT AND BEAUTIFUL AUTUMN LEAVES OF ALL SIZES BETWEEN PAGES OF HEAVY BOOKS. USE THESE LEAVES ON YOUR TABLE.

GATHER LONG STRANDS OF BITTERSWEET AND GRAPEVINES. YOU'LL FIND THESE VINES ALONG THE EDGE OF WOODLAND. THE BITTERSWEET HAS ORANGE RED BERRIES. TWIST THE VINES INTO A WREATH TO HANG ON THE KITCHEN DOOR.

RECORD THE COLORS AND LOCATION OF YOUR BLOOMING CHRYSANTHEMUMS. IN THE SPRING, WHEN YOU DIG THEM UP AND DIVIDE THEM, YOU CAN CHOOSE NEW GARDEN SPOTS WHERE THEY WILL COMPLEMENT THE COLORS AND TEXTURES OF OTHER FALL-BLOOMING PLANTS, LIKE ASTERS AND AUTUMN JOY SEDUM AND ALL THE ANNUALS THAT BLOOM UNTIL FROST.

89

One Gardener's Thanksgiving List

> It is good to say thank you to the Lord, to
> sing praises to the God who is above all gods.
> Every morning tell him, "Thank you for your
> kindness," and every evening rejoice in all his
> faithfulness.

PSALM 92:1-2, TLB

Because I'm a polite person, I usually say thank you when I am given
a gift. However, several times when I thanked someone for giving me a
plant out of her garden she said, "Never say thanks for a gift plant. It won't
grow if you say thanks!" *Why?* I wondered and still wonder. Who started
such a rumor? I don't believe it, and I have evidence to the contrary.

I want to cultivate and keep a thankful heart because God has given
me so much. I want to remain aware that all I have and enjoy is from my
heavenly Father, so I've made a list of things from my garden for which
I am thankful:

The foxglove and columbine that have reseeded themselves in
surprising places
That I can make a quick run out to the herb bed for chives and
tarragon for a recipe

A walk around the garden, with a cup of coffee in hand, to admire
things after three hours of weeding (Thank you, Lord, for energy
and a beautiful day's work.)

That the eighty-year-old Norway spruce
fell on our house (Well, maybe
not that it fell, but that it missed
the viburnum and the stone wall,
and no one was hurt); and that
my husband, who built this house
out of a barn, knows how to fix
the roof (Plus, now the *potager*
gets more sunlight on the west side
because the spruce is gone.)

The morning glories (Could there be a better name for that heavenly blue trumpet blossom that greets the morning with such joy
and proclaims the radiance of its Creator?)

The cosmos that I grew and picked for a vase on the dining-room table

The praying mantis, ladybugs, fireflies, and green lacewings that
I find in my garden (All these insects eat those other insects I
don't want, like slugs, aphids, and cutworms.)

The shallots and squash drying in the sun on the stone wall

The goldfinch that enjoys the sunflower seeds; the hummingbird that
visits the trumpet vine; the morning doves that drink from the pond

The rain that is soaking into the soil, softening the seeds and wash-
ing the broccoli

The muscles that ache after pulling out weeds (You, Lord, have
kept me healthy and strong this year.)

The seasons and the weather that each season brings— wind and rain and snow and sunshine; that God has allowed me to see more of his tender and wise working this year in my garden and in my life

It is a persistent conviction among people that to be in a garden is to be closer to God. And no wonder. God's delicate and strong work is

evident everywhere. Many people are moved to praise and thankfulness when they are surrounded by the beauty of a garden. If they don't know Christ Jesus, the Creator of it all, who will they thank? ❖

DIGGING DEEPER

Think of all the benefits of gardening, of all the opportunities a garden gives for sharing, meditation, exercise, and joy. For which are you most thankful? Make your own list of things for which you praise and thank the Lord. Maybe you could turn your list into a song to sing to the Lord.

PRAYER

Thank you, Lord, for making the world, for creating it with your children in mind. Thank you for causing the earth's systems to function with precision and beauty. You cause water to evaporate from the oceans and fall from the clouds as rain on the land. You make my garden grow. Thank you for all that you have given me.

GARDENING TIPS

PLANT GARLIC, SHALLOTS, AND MULTIPLIER ONIONS IN THE FALL FOR A BIGGER HARVEST IN THE SPRING. COVER THE PLANTING WITH A HEAVY MULCH TO PREVENT THE BULBS FROM LOOSENING AND LIFTING IN COLD WEATHER.

FROM MID-SEPTEMBER ON IS THE TIME TO HARVEST CARROTS, PARSNIPS, AND RUTABAGAS. OR YOU CAN LEAVE THEM IN THE GARDEN AND HARVEST THROUGHOUT THE WINTER. JUST PLACE SOME BALES OF STRAW OR A THICK LAYER OF MULCH OVER THE ROWS.

BRING SOME OF YOUR GARDEN INDOORS FOR THE WINTER. CUTTINGS OF BEGONIA, IMPATIENS, COLEUS, AND MANY OTHER PLANTS WILL ROOT IN A GLASS OF WATER ON A SUNNY WINDOWSILL. YOU CAN THEN PLANT THEM IN POTTING SOIL. THEY'LL CONTINUE TO GROW AND BLOOM AND CHEER YOU THROUGH THE COLD MONTHS.

Anticipation

Don't get tired of doing what is good. Don't get discouraged and give up, for we will reap a harvest of blessing at the appropriate time.

GALATIANS 6:9

Loaded down with nine bags of bulbs and the bulb planter, I head outside to perform an act of faith. I will spend the next few hours burying hundreds of bulbs. I'll make holes, plop the bulbs in right-side up, maybe add some bonemeal to the hole, and fill the hole up with soil. When I am through, I'll have nothing to show for it but empty bags and a sore back. I only know that those bulbs have the potential to transform. In the spring, at the proper time, I'll see the result of my work, the reward of my faith in those papery globes that I buried. Crowds of daffodils and drifts of pink, purple, and white tulips will rise up in the garden.

Gardening is an act of faith. We bend down and bury seeds, bulbs, corms, and tubers. We plant and water and hope for results. We believe that we will reap what we've sown.

When we plant seeds, it's usually during the pleasant springtime. The chore of sowing is speeded along by the sun's growing stronger and getting higher in the sky. And with seeds, the results are quick. In a week or two, new life sprouts up and justifies our faith. But planting bulbs as flowers are dying all around us in the garden takes *real* faith! There's a chill in the air and a long wait ahead.

Doing good to others can resemble the act of planting bulbs. God says he can use our acts of kindness and love to produce a harvest of blessing in the lives of others. A little bulb of kindness planted in someone's life can turn into a flower of faith in that person's heart. But he also says it may take a long time to see the results of our doing what is good.

So we have need of patience, a quality the Holy Spirit desires to produce in us. We may think that we need patience with our own faults or those of others that annoy us. But patience can also be called quiet anticipation. Patience is faith waiting for God to act, to do what he has promised.

And what God has promised is that he will make use of every good thing we do for him. When we share each other's troubles or try to help someone who has sinned to get back on track with God, the Lord makes our loving acts grow into something bigger than our deeds. He causes new life to sprout in people's hearts. He blesses their lives, and ours, with more faith, thankfulness, and joy.

No matter how many bulbs I plant each fall, when spring comes, I wish I had planted more. So when I want to give up planting bulbs because the wind is cold and the earth is damp and my back says stop, I can look ahead to what each bulb will produce. In the spring I will see that the results of all that digging on that cold day months ago far exceed what I had anticipated.

And every bulb I plant can remind me that God keeps his promises. He tells me to keep going in my work for him, in my attempts to show love to him by loving and serving others. The results are sure to come right on time. ✣

DIGGING DEEPER

Take a moment to read Galatians 5:22–6:10 and 1 Corinthians 15:58. What kinds of deeds come to mind when you think of "doing good"? Note that the verse in 1 Corinthians (TLB) urges us to "abound" in doing good. How does the word *abound* affect your understanding of how the Lord wants us to live?

PRAYER

Lord, give me eyes to see people in need. Help me to allow your Spirit to produce fruit in me so I may not get discouraged but will abound in doing what pleases you.

Gardening Tips

Plant narcissus where they can "naturalize," that is, spread, and not have to be moved when they multiply. A good place for narcissus is on the edge of your garden, under deciduous trees, along the edge of a wooded area, or scattered throughout the shrubbery border.

After the bulbs are finished flowering, their green leaves are manufacturing food for next year's bloom. So don't remove the leaves until they have turned brown. If you plant bulbs among ground covers like periwinkle, ferns, and pachysandra, the bulbs' fading leaves will be hidden somewhat.

The Latin name for sage is <u>salvia</u>, meaning "salvation." To make a sage wreath, cover a straw form with clusters of sage, using old-fashioned hairpins or pieces of bent wire to fix the bunches to the form. Add some dusty miller, feverfew, dried grasses, strawflowers, rose hips, and any other plant material you find in the fall garden.

> There is required patience on our part, till the summer-fruit in heaven be ripe for us. It is in the bud; but there be many things to do before our harvest come. —Samuel Rutherford

WINTER

The Garden Surrenders

In winter we look up.
The earth is leaf-littered so
we look up and watch the
snow fall.
Ice crystals on branches and bare
trees against a steel sky
claim our eyes.
We look up and
see the stars.   J.S.

Life's Little Joys

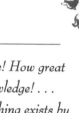

*Oh, what a wonderful God we have! How great
are his riches and wisdom and knowledge! . . .
Everything comes from him; everything exists by
his power and is intended for his glory.*

ROMANS 11:33, 36

Do you own a *leuchtlupe?* The garden writer Allen Lacy, in his book, *The
Gardener's Eye,* suggests getting one. It is a hand lens with a strong beam of
light that illuminates an object and magnifies it ten times. It gives you an
insect's-eye view of flowers, leaves, and seeds, anything small. Mr. Lacy
describes a little snowdrop flower as seen through this lens:

> A snowdrop is as complex and subtle in its beauty as an orchid . . .
> the [three] outer petals enfold and partly conceal the inner ones.
> These are shorter by half. They overlap to form a tube, which flares
> outward near its end. The inner petals are pristine white near the
> base, then banded with a contrasting shade of fresh lime green, then
> edged again with a thin band of white. On closer look, the band of
> green is not a solid band at all: it is composed of very narrow verti-
> cal green stripes, separated by even more narrow stripes of white.
> (*The Gardener's Eye, and Other Essays.* New York: Atlantic Monthly Press, 1992)

When I also looked at a snowdrop under a lens, I saw a small blotch of delicate yellow above the green band on the inner petals, just where the edge of the petal was scalloped.

Allen Lacy put seeds under the hand lens and found that they resembled much larger things in the world. A scabiosa seed resembled a badminton birdie. Catnip seeds looked like little wide-eyed monkey faces.

It would be delightful, and time well spent, to walk around the garden with a hand lens, looking at blossoms and leaves and pebbles and even dirt. Think what glory, what surprises, lie just under our nose, under our feet.

Little things can magnify God. Being able to see the beauty in the tiny details of our garden enlarges our appreciation of God's power as well as his gentleness. Using the leuchtlupe is a fascinating way to see and appreciate the little joys and surprises that God has sprinkled all around us.

Is there a lens we could use to look at the details of our life—something to help us see the pattern in our circumstances, the character of God at work in the design of our days?

Perhaps this lens is a believing and expectant heart, a heart ready to worship and obey whatever God reveals to it. Such a heart approaches God's Word willingly, eager to see more of the Lord. Someone with such a heart is always watchful for glimpses of the Lord's working. She may keep track of what the Lord is saying by recording verses that speak to her from the Word day by day. By meditating on these verses, she can discern direction from God. This watchful heart is often joyful because it frequently catches sight of some good thing God has done, some small wonder God has performed for his children.

God is in the details. Something of the Creator is visible in every-

thing, every little thing, he has made. All created things are intended for God's glory, so the more we can see of them, the greater will be our ability to worship and praise him. And everything God does in us is because of his love for us. It is all for our joy. When we believe this, we will recognize the hand of the Lord in the details of our life, and our joy will be full. ✢

DIGGING DEEPER

Through what "lens" have you been able to see what the Lord is doing? Do the details of your life bring you joy or do they cause you to question God's love? Ask the Lord for the ability to believe in his tender love for you. Ask him to restore your joy and show you a small wonder, made just for you.

PRAYER

Dear Lord, thank you for the little joys that I find in my life. Thank you for the things that cheer me when my heart is heavy—like tiny snowdrops or a surprise visit from a dear friend. Thank you that these happy things are gifts from you to deepen my worship of you, my Creator.

Gardening Tips

Snowdrops (<u>Galanthus nivalis</u>) are the first flowers to appear in late winter. They will even push through a light snowfall and bloom in the snow. Plant snowdrop bulbs in the fall, near a window, so you can watch for their arrival in February.

Shirley poppies are small, fleeting beauties in the garden but worth having for the sheer beauty of their translucent petals trembling in the breeze and their clear, delicate colors. If you sow shirley poppy seeds every few weeks in the spring, you'll have these lovely flowers all summer and into fall. Sow directly where you want them to grow. The poppies will reseed themselves and give you flowers again next year.

A Blanket for the Garden

*Most important of all, continue to show deep
love for each other, for love covers a multitude
of sins.*

1 PETER 4:8

The leaves on the trees died in splendor. Now they litter the lawn
with patches of brown. It is December, and the garden surrenders to the
shortened days and the frost. Until the ground freezes hard, I run around
tucking crocus bulbs into bare spots under trees and other places that I
will eventually forget. The crocus blossoms will surprise me come spring.
Finally, I put the garden to bed for the winter under a thick blanket of
mulch.

Since we have so many trees on our hill, I have all the leaf mulch I
can use. I pile up the dry, crushed leaves around the roses. I dump loads
of leaves in the *potager.* I rake them off the lawn and onto the flower
beds. Now all is brown on our hill, except for the evergreens, which are
my tonic against color deprivation.

Eventually, God puts another blanket on the garden—snow!

Snow is good for gardens in the northern temperate zone. It protects the soil from the strong winter winds that dry out the topsoil and blow it away. Plants are kept snug under snow, safe from the stress of freezing and thawing. And as the snow gradually thaws, it improves the soil's texture.

The deep snow covers the brown deadness in the garden. Dry spikes and sticks and leftover rubble are blanketed with a gentleness that softens all the sharp edges. The garden is beautiful and clean again. Gone are all the mistakes of last season's planting and neglect. Faded grass and weeds disappear. The blanket of snow hides the piles of dirt on the lawn where the dog was digging for moles. Thanks to the snow, the garden and I must rest and gather strength for the next growing season.

The deep pristine snow blanketing the garden is a picture of the love of God. God has covered our sins completely with the blood of his Son. No matter how deep the stain of our sins, God's love is deeper. It removes the stain and makes us as clean as the newly fallen snow. In Christ, God has given us absolute forgiveness and acceptance.

Think what our love for one another can be when it is modeled after the love of God. Our love will be full of forgiveness. This forgiving love will look for a way to smooth out the rough spots in a relationship. It will cover over any wrongs that might have been done to us. It will take no more notice. This deep love will persist in believing in the other person. It will give hope for a fresh start after a failure and will be patient during growth and improvement. Anyone who receives this kind of love from us will feel safe around us and be able to enjoy the freedom of forgiveness. We will have harmony in our relationships and experience lighthearted yet deep friendships.

A new snowfall always delights us. We love the way it brings a peace and beauty to our world, the way it slows down our schedule and brings out the playful side of everyone. When you next enjoy a deep snow falling on your garden or see a picture of snow-covered gardens, let it also be a reminder of the deep love of God for you and of the kind of love we are to have for the people in our life. ✢

DIGGING DEEPER

When have you found it hard to express this deep, covering kind of love? If you began today to love someone like Jesus loves you, what changes would take place?

PRAYER

Thank you, God, that I am cleansed from my sin and made white as snow by the blood of Christ. Thank you that your love for me is deep and eternal. Help me to love others the way you love me.

Gardening Tips

Leaves used as mulch can be put through a mulcher or chopped by running the lawn mower over them a few times. This way the leaves will decompose more rapidly and won't smother emerging plants in the spring.

If you have too many leaves, you could bag the leaves, add a handful of manure, sprinkle some water in with them, close up the bag, and poke a few holes in the sides. Now throw these bags anywhere out of sight—under a bush, behind a shed—or place them over weedy areas in the garden. If you think of it, you can turn them over a few times during the year. Come spring, the weeds will be smothered, and the leaves will have decomposed and be ready to use as compost.

Catalogues and Dreams

Now you have every spiritual gift you need as you eagerly wait for the return of our Lord Jesus Christ.

1 CORINTHIANS 1:7

They're slick and beautiful. They appeal to my greed and passion. They've got me hooked. I'm talking about gardening and seed catalogues. Whenever a new one arrives, and it seems like it's every other day during the winter months, I drop what I'm doing and sit down to read and dream.

My son got hooked, too. After six years in the navy, he was finally finished with gray paint and the smell of sweaty men in tight quarters. He came home from the sea, hungry for beauty, color, and fragrance. He saw my catalogues and wanted a rose garden.

So he and I walked around our hill, looking for the perfect place to plant roses. Then he spread armfuls of catalogues on the dining-room table and spent days dreaming and choosing. He finally placed his order for ten bushes, ones with gorgeous colors and lots of fragrance. After all, he said, if it doesn't smell good, it's not a real rose. He kept the catalogues handy so we could see the pictures of the beauties that would arrive at our door. And we waited. The wait was worth it, however. A year after my son planted the rose bushes, we had armfuls of roses to decorate the tables at his wedding reception.

Waiting is another word for winter. During the long dark days, I wait for my flower and vegetable seeds to come in the mail. I keep checking on the branches of forsythia in a vase on the windowsill, waiting for their gold flowers to appear. I wait for the ground outside to soften enough so that I can plant peas.

The catalogue pictures and the dreams of our garden-to-be are what keep many of us gardeners looking forward eagerly. This is just what the Word of God can do for us as Christians. As we read, we imagine what it will be like when this world is ended and eternity begins: the end of sorrow and decay; living forever in the light of the glory of God; being with all of our brothers and sisters in Christ.

As we discover more of Christ's beauty and love, we get excited about seeing him face-to-face. We see that we will finally be all that we were meant to be. When he appears, the apostle John says, "we shall be like him, for we shall see him as he is. Everyone who has this hope in him purifies himself, just as he is pure" (1 John 3:2-3, NIV).

Waiting eagerly does a work in us that will be completed when all the waiting is over. We begin to rest in the fact of Christ's complete

forgiveness, and our dread and guilt are replaced by lighthearted hope. Our eagerness gives us energy. Hard times become endurable because we have our eyes on what is sure to come—on who is sure to arrive—maybe today. ❖

To what do you look forward with eager anticipation? How will you pass the time waiting for Jesus to return? What changes would take place in your thoughts and actions if you waited *eagerly* every day for Jesus Christ to appear?

PRAYER

Lord, thank you for the promise of your return. Please do your transforming work in me so that I may not be ashamed when you appear but will be ready and eager for your coming.

Gardening Tips

If you have flower and vegetable seeds left over from last year, you can still use them this year if you have stored them properly. Extra seed should be kept in air-tight containers in a cool dry place. Small film canisters make handy storage containers for seeds. Be sure to label them. The seeds will stay good for several years.

If you are in doubt about some seeds, you can test them to see if they are still viable. Sprinkle a dozen or so seeds on a moist half-sheet of paper towel, fold this in half and put the towel into a plastic sandwich bag and seal it. Let it lie flat for a few days, then check to see if any seed has sprouted. If not, add a little water if the towel seems a bit dry and wait a few days more, then check again. If most of the seeds have sprouted, you may use the rest of them this year. You can even plant the ones you have sprouted if you do it right away.

Diligence versus the Deer

Even though the fig trees have no blossoms, and there are no grapes on the vine; even though the olive crop fails, and the fields lie empty and barren; even though the flocks die in the fields, and the cattle barns are empty, yet I will rejoice in the Lord! I will be joyful in the God of my salvation. The Sovereign Lord is my strength!

HABAKKUK 3:17-19

I love to dream about how my garden is going to look—just perfect, of course. But reality can be a rude awakening. Here are some entries from my gardening journal (mercifully not all from the same year):

March 10—The six Fraser firs that we planted as saplings at the bottom of our hill have finally reached six feet in height; the deer stripped them of half of their branches last night by rubbing their antlers on them.

April 6—Hordes of aphids in the greenhouse, ruining the lettuce; spent $10 last week on lacewing larvae, which are supposed to eat the aphids; can't find a single lacewing larva today; still plenty of aphids.

August 19—Plague of bean beetles; fuzzy yellow larvae all over the leaves that remain; plants all skinny and naked.

Only public gardens and gardens of the rich can look nearly perfect all the time. They have a large staff and a bankroll to match. I do have my husband, though. He runs the tiller through the *potager*. He trims the privet hedge that surrounds it. He does the heavy digging and weeding when the bittersweet and poison ivy run rampant.

But there's always some grass ruining the trim edge of a flower bed or huge and sinister-looking weeds showing up in the perennial border seemingly overnight. And there's the new puppy who thinks life's a lark and everything in the world exists for him to attack and chew. And I might as well mention again the beautiful yet pesty deer who ate thirty-one rosebuds last week. These are the sad consequences of living on a large property and being an overachiever in the garden. There's just no way I can fix all the problems and get the vegetable and flower beds looking good all at once.

Still I don't give up. Next year, I say, I'll do better. I'll apply diligence and perseverance: I'll weed more often; I'll get lion dung from the zoo to scare away the deer; I'll start more seedlings to replace what was lost. . . . Gardeners are such hopeful people.

My daily life has its share of disappointments, too. I catch a bad cold just when my workload is the heaviest. My freezer quits the day after I've finished pitting and freezing the cherry harvest. With the disappointments that come

113

with gardening, and in daily living, I can only keep going by acknowledging the Lord in the process.

When I walk through the gate into my *potager,* the Lord and I go in together. I expect to revel in some sweet discovery—the strawberries ripening, a surprise flower seedling looking at home among the onions, lettuces as lovely as roses. All these things I take as gifts from my gardener Father in heaven. I'll find signs of stress, too—a cherished plant uprooted and withered in the sun or a whole row of planted seed that did not germinate. Learning to accept these small trials in the garden helps me to accept life's

 disappointments, too. Acceptance keeps hope from dying. Acceptance is not mere submission; it is saying yes to God's sovereignty in the daily things and in the garden.

As I read God's Word, his Spirit teaches me to live by hope and not give up. He keeps telling me that his presence, his love, and his strength are available to meet the disappointments and to learn from them. God always has more to give—more of himself and more lessons from a less-than-perfect garden. ✣

DIGGING DEEPER

How do you deal with the small disappointments of life? Do you find it easy or hard to "rejoice in the Lord always"? Why? When Habbakuk rejoiced, he was reminded of God's strength on his behalf, and his heart was encouraged. So we, too, can choose to rejoice, not because our days run smoothly, but because of who God is.

114

PRAYER

Lord, my life is like an imperfect garden. There are so many delightful things for which I thank you, but there are also failures and disappointments.

Help me, Lord, to recognize your hand in all these things, to accept your work in my life, and to rejoice anyway because you are the God of my salvation.

GARDENING TIPS

YOU MIGHT CONSIDER KEEPING TRACK OF YOUR GARDENING SUCCESSES IN A GARDENING JOURNAL IF YOU'RE NOT CURRENTLY DOING SO. RECORD THE WEATHER, BLOOM AND HARVEST DATES, AND THE NAMES OF SEED VARIETIES YOU ENJOY. TAKE PICTURES OF YOUR GARDEN EACH SEASON AND KEEP THESE IN THE JOURNAL, TOO. GARDENING JOURNALS ARE AVAILABLE AT BOOKSTORES, BUT YOU CAN MAKE YOUR OWN, USING A HARDBACK, LINED BLANK BOOK.

THE LARGE SEEDS OF PEAS AND CORN GERMINATE BETTER IF THEY ARE SOAKED OVERNIGHT IN WATER BEFORE PLANTING. TINY SEEDS, LIKE THOSE OF CARROTS AND LETTUCE, AND MANY FLOWER SEEDS NEED CONSTANT MOIS-TURE TO GERMINATE BUT MUST NOT BE PLANTED VERY DEEP. AFTER YOU SCATTER THE SEEDS IN THE ROW AND SPRINKLE FINE SOIL OVER THEM, WATER GENTLY BUT THOROUGHLY. KEEP THE SEEDBED MOIST UNTIL THE SEEDS HAVE SPROUTED.

115

In the Greenhouse

God knows how much I love you and long for
you with the tender compassion of Christ Jesus.
I pray that your love for each other will overflow
more and more, and that you will keep on
growing in your knowledge and understanding.

PHILIPPIANS 1:8-9

My husband and son built a greenhouse for me out of recycled glass doors and new lumber. I often sit in my greenhouse to read and write, enjoying the earthy smell and the warmth. On late winter days, when the weather is windy and cold, and the outside temperature is thirty-six degrees, inside the greenhouse, it is a snug seventy-five or eighty degrees.

Thanks to the greenhouse, we can enjoy fresh spinach and lettuce in January and February. I can start seeds of annuals and vegetables and get a head start on the growing season.

Plants that start their lives in the greenhouse have to be weaned from their sheltered lifestyle before they can be moved outside to their spot in the garden. This is called "hardening off," which means the young plants have to be gradually introduced to the stronger air currents, wind, rain, and full sun. I have to put the potted plants outside during the day and bring them in at night for a week or so until the stems and leaves have toughened up.

All new Christians need regular and personal care for a while, just like my greenhouse plants. God wants his children to grow strong and hardy, able to live in the real world as fruitful Christians. He desires older Christians to care for younger ones and to show them how to put their roots down deep into the love of God.

When I was a very young Christian, a more mature Christian woman took me under her care and began to share her life with me. She made time for me, prayed with me and for me, and helped me to begin to grow in following Christ. She taught me how to study the Bible and helped me to set goals for my life that would move me closer to Christ.

Now this dear friend knew that she was not solely responsible for my growth. When I received God's gift of eternal life in Jesus Christ, his Holy Spirit took up residence in me. He became my teacher and guide. And the local body of believers in Christ was there to provide fellowship and teaching and communal worship. But God wanted me to have some personal care; so, he gave me the gift of my friend. She loved me, and her love compelled her to care for my needs and teach me how to be stronger as a Christian. She honestly shared her weaknesses as well as her triumphs. Now, many years later, I try to follow her example by seeking out young Christians who would welcome some personal encouragement and instruction.

My greenhouse is a place to start seeds growing and to nurture them to the point where they can stand on their own in the garden. I do what it takes to help them become hardy plants that will mature and produce flowers and vegetables. In the same way, we can provide a nurturing relationship for a new believer in Christ who comes our way. Simple things seem

to work the best as we seek to encourage growth in someone's life: sharing a meal and having a listening heart; giving a copy of a favorite book or recording that has encouraged us; taking a walk together and talking about what we enjoy and what is hard for us as we seek to follow Christ. We can be effective helpers of another's growth, not because of how much we know, but because of Who we know.

When we seek to help a young Christian grow in Christ, we become partners with God, who desires that all of us grow in Christlikeness. We may form friendships that last for many years. And we will see the fruit of our labor when those we've helped begin to help others. ✤

DIGGING DEEPER

What has helped you as you sought to follow Christ? Who are your "heroes" (in the Bible or in books you've read or perhaps someone you know)? How have these people blessed your life? Can you think of anyone who might benefit from what you can share?

PRAYER

I thank you, Lord, for those people who have nurtured me in my walk with you, who cared for me with your kind of encouraging and exhorting love. Help me to be aware of those who need personal help and encouragement. And show me how to help them grow toward you.

Gardening Tips

A cold frame is a minigreenhouse. To build one, you'll need a window frame, preferably wood with glass intact, or a storm window or large pane of glass. Build a box the same size as the window or glass out of two-by-six-foot or two-by-eight-foot boards. Position this box on the south side of your house or garden, directly on the soil. Raise the back of the box up a bit with soil or bricks so the window frame cover tilts toward the sun. Bank up the soil around the outside of the box. Add some more soil to the inside of the box so that the soil level tilts on the same angle as the window frame. You can add hinges, too, to attach the window frame to the box. (Adapted from Mel Bartholomew, <u>Square Foot Gardening</u>, Emmaus, Pa.: Rodale Press, 1981.)

A Garden
Meditation

*Every day Jesus went to the Temple to
teach, and each evening he returned to spend the
night on the Mount of Olives.*

LUKE 21:37

The word *garden* conjures up all kinds of green images, of things growing beautifully. When we walk through the garden gate, we anticipate
sweet air and enchantment. We know somehow that being there in the
garden is good for us. We expect to see order of the most pleasing kind.
There will be rows of cabbages and peas or plots of daisies and irises.
There will be a place to sit and wonder. We don't expect to find clamor
or agitated motion.

Solitude. Beauty. Stillness. All of these we find in a garden. This is why
Jesus chose a garden so often for his private moments with God, his Father.

In the last year of Jesus' life on earth, he spent many hours on the
Mount of Olives. The mount was really a large area of many gardens or
tended groves. Besides olive groves (which Vincent Van Gogh once
described as too beautiful to try to paint), there were fig trees, pine, palm
and myrtle. This lovely elevated place was probably used by many as a
"resort," to get away from the hot, crowded streets of Jerusalem. The

mount was the regular meeting place for Jesus and his disciples. At the foot of the mount is the Garden of Gethsemane.

Jesus Christ often sought solitude and rest on the mount. I can imagine that he sometimes encountered gardeners hard at work there. Did these gardeners know that the beauty they were creating and tending was being enjoyed by the Son of God?

During the last week of his life, Jesus spent every night on the mount, in those gardens. He found there the privacy he needed to pour out his soul in submission to his Father. He was buried in a garden, and after his resurrection, he was first seen there by Mary (see John 20:11-18).

Mary thought Jesus was the gardener. Why? Had he stooped to admire a plant or pull a weed? Did it appear that he felt right at home? Probably Mary just didn't expect to see anyone else there at that early hour except the gardener. The text simply says she saw someone standing behind her and thought it was the gardener. Perhaps he had been walking there, enjoying its quiet beauty, just as he might have done before his death.

God is, of course, the first to have designed a garden. It was the first home for the first man and woman, who were the first gardeners (Gen. 2:8). Perhaps our love of gardens is also a remembrance and celebration of our origins. That garden in Eden had two main features: a collection

of fruit trees and a river. God chose the site, planned and planted it himself, with people in mind. He walked there and sought intimate companionship there with the people he had made.

Today, in our fast-paced, hectic world, a garden can provide the relief our soul needs. It can provide a place to be quiet, to think and seek God's

presence. Even a window ledge where we have gathered some pretty pots of blooms and greenery can become for us a retreat.

We can draw up a chair, sit and enjoy the freshness of our plants, and relax. We can keep our Bibles near that window garden and make it our meeting place with the Lord.

Are we nearer God's heart in a garden? We can be if that is what we seek. ✤

DIGGING DEEPER

What do you enjoy most about your garden? What do you think about the most when you are in your garden? How has God met you there? Is there someone you know who doesn't have a garden with whom you could share your little plot of beauty and quiet?

PRAYER

I know you have blessed me, Father, with space to make a large garden. Thank you for making things grow, for the beauty that happens in my garden far beyond my talent and effort. Keep me alert to ways I can share my garden with others who need its blessings.

Gardening Tips

If you have success growing African violets on your windowsill, you can grow an orchid! Phalaenopsis, commonly called "Moth orchid," is easy to care for, requiring the same light and plant food as violets. Moth orchids have dark green, thick, strappy leaves and grow best in orchid "soil," which is a mixture of moss and charcoal and wood chips. You can purchase this mixture ready to use. These orchid plants bloom once a year but are thrilling to watch week after week as the blossoms develop. Once in flower, the blossoms can last for months.

Garden Words, God's Word

*All Scripture is inspired by God and is useful to
teach us what is true and to make us realize
what is wrong in our lives. It straightens us out
and teaches us to do what is right. It is God's
way of preparing us in every way, fully equipped
for every good thing God wants us to do.*

2 TIMOTHY 3:16-17

Winter is the time for gardeners to read. Those of us who live
in areas with cold winters know that there's nothing much to be
done in the garden, except to gather fallen branches or shake heavy
snow off the evergreens. This is the time to put a fire in the stove,
make a cup of hot chocolate, and sit down with a stack of garden
books.

What is it about gardening books that makes them so appealing?
The books I choose either have lots of photographs or are written so
well that I think I'd want to read them even if I weren't a gardener. Do
I hope to stimulate my creativity or just indulge my craving for color-
ful garden life? For both reasons I carry home armfuls of these books
from the library every few weeks.

I know I won't remember all the tips and instructions I read each winter. I only hope that some of those tips will sink into my mind so I can draw on them later. What happens more frequently as I go through these books is I get ideas. I see the English cottage gardens, for instance, and I long to create that homey crowded look in my Maryland garden. I see how perennials are arranged so that they are blooming in sync with each other, and I'm challenged to try such a planting myself.

I have found that many writers and poets are also enthusiastic gardeners. I read their books and discover that my thoughts and feelings about gardening are shared by many.

Some people enjoy reading about gardening while not having or even wanting to have a garden. I identify with their love of beautiful and well-written books. To immerse oneself in a good book is to take a journey on the words of others and discover these words were written with you in mind.

When we read the Word of God, we go on a different kind of journey, sometimes pleasurable, sometimes disturbing. The Bible is the most thrilling, the most puzzling, the most heart-grabbing collection of books there is. We find our thoughts written down on its pages. In the Psalms we read about ourselves—our struggles, our questions, as well as our praise. The Gospels draw us into the circle surrounding our Savior, and we watch him move among the people, teaching, healing, astounding them. Men and women in the Scriptures instruct and encourage us by their failures and victories as they attempt to follow God.

But we are often confronted by the truths of God's Word, not merely entertained or intrigued. We read and see a need for change in ourselves. We realize our need to worship and obey the God whose Word it is.

Just about everything you want to know about gardening has been written down. Find the right book, read it, and you'll know what to 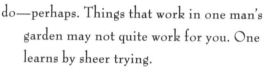 do—perhaps. Things that work in one man's garden may not quite work for you. One learns by sheer trying.

All that we need to know about living God's way is written in the Word of God. It is perfectly suited to every heart everywhere, all the time. It is ours to read and weep over, ours to enjoy. God's words comfort us and show us how much he loves us. And his Word is ours to obey so that we may become more like Christ and do those things God has for us to do. ✣

DIGGING DEEPER

How has God's Word helped you in the past? What passage would you share with a friend if you had the chance? Why? Do you have a plan to help you read the Bible regularly? Ask the Lord for a love for his Word, an understanding of it, and the will to obey what he shows you.

PRAYER

Consider praying the Scriptures. For example: Open my eyes to see the wonderful truths in your law. . . . Teach me, O Lord, to follow every one of your principles. Give me understanding and I will obey your law; I will put it into practice with all my heart. Make me walk along the path of your commands, for that is where my happiness is found (Ps. 119:18, 33-35).

GARDENING TIPS

SOME FAVORITE GARDEN WRITERS:

ELIZABETH LAWRENCE, <u>THROUGH THE GARDEN GATE</u>. EDITED BY BILL NEAL. CHAPEL HILL: UNIVERSITY OF NORTH CAROLINA PRESS, 1990.

CHERRY LEWIS, EDITOR, <u>THE MAKING OF A GARDEN</u> (AN ANTHOLOGY OF GERTRUDE JEKYLL'S WRITINGS). ANTIQUE COLLECTORS' CLUB, LTD. WOODBRIDGE, SUFFOLK, ENGLAND: BARON PUBLISHING, 1985.

HENRY MITCHELL, <u>ONE MAN'S GARDEN</u>. BOSTON: HOUGHTON MIFFLIN CO., 1992.

ELEANOR PERENYI, <u>GREEN THOUGHTS</u>. NEW YORK: RANDOM HOUSE, 1981.

ROGER B. SWAIN, <u>THE PRACTICAL GARDENER: A GUIDE TO BREAKING NEW GROUND</u>. BOSTON: LITTLE, BROWN AND CO., 1989.

PATRICIA THORPE, <u>GROWING PAINS</u>. SAN DIEGO: HARCOURT BRACE AND CO., 1994.

127

ANNA B. WARNER, <u>GARDENING BY MYSELF: CENTENNIAL EDITION.</u>
WEST POINT, N.Y.: THE CONSTITUTION ISLAND ASSOCIATION,
1972.

HOW EXQUISITE THE UNBENDING OF NATURE! EVEN WITH
ICE AND SNOW STILL IN SIGHT, THERE IS A CHANGE IN THE
WHOLE LOOK OF THE WORLD. THE LIGHT IS DIFFERENT,
AND MORE TENDER; THE CLOUDS ROLL UP IN SOFTER
LINES; AND IN THE WIND THERE COMES THE STRANGE
WILD SCENT OF SWELLING BUDS.

EXTREMES MEET AND THE ECHO OF DEPARTING WHEELS
GIVES PLACE TO THE FAINT ROLL OF THE APPROACHING
AND THE DAYS OF LOSS PASS GENTLY ON INTO DAYS OF
HOPE.

—ANNA B. WARNER, GARDENING BY MYSELF